CITYSPOTS
ST PETERSBURG

WHAT'S IN YOUR GUIDEBOOK?

Independent authors Impartial up-to-date information from our travel experts who meticulously source local knowledge.

Experience Thomas Cook's 165 years in the travel industry and guidebook publishing enriches every word with expertise you can trust.

Travel know-how Contributions by thousands of staff around the globe, each one living and breathing travel.

Editors Travel-publishing professionals, pulling everything together to craft a perfect blend of words, pictures, maps and design.

You, the traveller We deliver a practical, no-nonsense approach to information, geared to how you really use it.

CITYSPOTS
ST PETERSBURG

Ryan Levitt

Written by Ryan Levitt
Original photography by Neil Setchfield
Front cover photography (Church on Spilled Blood) © Ellen Rooney / Getty Images
Series design based on an original concept by Studio 183 Limited

Produced by Cambridge Publishing Management Limited
Project Editor: Penny Isaac
Layout: Natalie White
Maps: PC Graphics
Transport map: © Communicarta Limited

Published by Thomas Cook Publishing
A division of Thomas Cook Tour Operations Limited
Company Registration No. 1450464 England
PO Box 227, Unit 18, Coningsby Road
Peterborough PE3 8SB, United Kingdom
email: books@thomascook.com
www.thomascookpublishing.com
+ 44 (0) 1733 416477
ISBN-13: 978-1-84157-755-5

First edition © 2007 Thomas Cook Publishing
Text © 2007 Thomas Cook Publishing
Maps © 2007 Thomas Cook Publishing
Series Editor: Kelly Anne Pipes
Project Editor: Karen Fitzpatrick
Production/DTP: Steven Collins

Printed and bound in Spain by GraphyCems

CONTENTS

SYMBOLS KEY

The following symbols are used throughout this book:

ⓐ address ☎ telephone ⓦ website address ⓔ email
🕐 opening times Ⓝ public transport connections ⓘ important

The following symbols are used on the maps:

🖅	information office	O	city
✈	airport	O	large town
➕	hospital	o	small town
🛡	police station	=	motorway
🚌	bus station	—	main road
🚆	railway station	—	minor road
Ⓜ	metro	—	railway
✝	cathedral		

❶ numbers denote featured cafés & restaurants

Hotels and restaurants are graded by approximate price as follows:
£ budget ££ mid-range £££ expensive

---

❶ *The magnificent dome of St Isaac's Cathedral*

Introduction

Russia's second-largest city is first in the hearts of its population due to its collection of showpiece museums, elegant pastel-hued palaces, tree-lined parks and boulevards, not to mention its proud history of decadence and defiance.

Home to the Russian tsars for over three hundred years, St Petersburg has seen more than its share of political power struggles since it was founded on the banks of the Neva river by Peter the Great in 1703. Sheer determination built this city up to become the fourth largest in Europe within a century of its founding – and it's also what got its citizens through such moments as the storming of the Winter Palace by Communist revolutionaries and the two-and-a-half year blockade by the Nazis during World War II.

Look into the eyes of any local and you will see a mix of defiance, pride and despair. They defy you to think that any city is more beautiful. They take pride in the fact that they live in such an inspiring location. And they despair that years of Communist mismanagement have scarred the great city's inherent beauty.

A visit to St Petersburg will intoxicate and captivate you. As a city for romance, there are few rivals. Whether it's a summer night flooded with late sunlight – the so-called White Nights – along the banks of the river, or a winter's evening sharing a bottle of Georgian wine in a basement bar next to a cosy fireplace, you're sure to find your perfect corner. So take a stroll down Nevsky Prospekt and enjoy a caviar-covered *bliny*. I bet you'll never want to say *da svidaniya* (goodbye).

The Admiralty: one of the city's showpiece buildings

When to go

St Petersburg is a great city to visit at any time of the year, as long as you are prepared. Summer is the obvious time to plan a visit – but it is also the season when most visitors schedule a stay. Hotel room rates skyrocket by as much as 30 per cent during this time and your chances to meet and mix with locals diminishes. The most expensive period occurs during the White Nights festival; however, the excitement can make up for the additional expense if partying is in your blood. Spring and autumn waver climatically and can be hit or miss. Days are usually clear and cloudless, but when the rain does arrive it can hover for long periods.

Winter is the slowest time of year, as snowstorms pound the city and temperatures drop well below freezing. Locals are used to dealing with the winter extremes and know how to get by. You will, however, need to bundle up if you want to go exploring. Don't leave skin exposed for too long during the freezing months of January or February as frostbite can occur in minutes. Luckily, a shot of vodka and a warm bar will do much to produce a pleasant glow.

SEASONS & CLIMATE

St Petersburg's location on the Gulf of Finland is the principal reason that the city stays warmer than it should. A city this far north should be much colder, yet locals are blessed with a more temperate climate than other locations further inland on the same latitude. That's not to say that St Petersburg doesn't get cold. In the winter, temperatures can plummet. The average temperature in January is −8°C (17.6°F). The wind chill can make this feel much colder. As the cold is relatively dry, good heating and warm clothes do much to cut through the bitterness.

Summer takes its time to hit St Petersburg, arriving as late as mid-May. When it does come, temperatures can rise to as high as 20°C (68°F). July and August can bring even hotter weather, with humidity forcing many residents to the cooler climes of the Gulf beaches or countryside.

⬤ The colonnades of Gostiny Dvor provide shelter from inclement weather

ANNUAL EVENTS

In St Petersburg and the surrounding region there are many more events than can be mentioned here. Due to a lack of good websites and tourist boards, it can be difficult to keep track of dates, so contact your hotel's concierge when you make a booking to ensure you're in town when a celebration occurs.

March

International Women's Day Almost like a Communist version of Valentine's Day, this holiday sees women given gifts of chocolate and flowers. All businesses are shut to accommodate the romance.

April

Orthodox Easter Dates vary from the Gregorian calendar and usually fall a little after the Protestant and Catholic dates – but not always. Banners are hung outside every church celebrating the holiday, while midnight mass brings the hordes out on Easter eve.

June

Beer Festival This new addition to the festival scene is now one of the most popular in St Petersburg. Dates change every year, but it is usually held sometime around mid-June in the Peter & Paul Fortress. It's basically an excuse to drink lots of beer.

November

Day of Reconciliation and Accord National holiday held on the anniversary of the Revolution. Demonstrations and parades celebrating the 'good old days' are common.

PUBLIC HOLIDAYS
New Year's Day 1 January
Russian Orthodox Christmas Day 7 January
Defenders of the Motherland Day 23 February
International Women's Day 8 March
Easter Monday March/April
International Labour Day/Spring Festival 1 & 2 May
Victory Day 9 May
Russian Independence Day 12 June
Day of Reconciliation and Accord 7 November
Constitution Day 12 December

WHITE NIGHTS
When summer arrives, locals truly know how to take advantage of the warmer and sunnier weather. Off go the woollen scarves, fur hats and parkas, and on go the smiles, usually assisted by numerous shots of vodka.

The best (and wildest) time to experience this carefree period is during the White Nights Festival, which is held through the last two weeks of June and into early July. The term White Nights came from the fact that, because the city's latitude is so far north, this ensures that the sun stays up for an extraordinary length of time in and around the summer solstice. Locals party all day and during the (short) night, flooding the streets that surround Nevsky Prospekt and the Neva embankment. Depending on the sun's schedule, everything comes to a peak on the day of the White Nights carnival – however, there are plenty of other activities to keep visitors occupied.

Fans of high culture will love the fact that the Festival of Festivals international film celebration occurs during this time, in addition to the Stars of the White Nights Festival. The film festival rarely draws big names or stages grand premieres, but it does give film buffs a nice opportunity to catch Russian arthouse works that may not see the light of day outside the country.

Much more enticing in terms of glitterati is the Stars of the White Nights Festival, held at the Mariinsky, Hermitage and Conservatoire theatres. World-renowned performers flock to this celebration of opera and ballet, ending with the Tsarskoe Selo Carnival on the last weekend of June at the palace of the same name.

For details of what is happening on a day-by-day basis, check out the listings posted in the *St Petersburg Times* or *Where St Petersburg*, available free of charge throughout the city. Otherwise, keep your eyes peeled for flyers and street banners that advertise impromptu celebrations and performances.

December
Arts Square Winter Festival Orchestral works and classical and contemporary opera are performed during this month-long annual festival, considered by locals to be a highlight of the musical calendar. Every year boasts a different theme by which the programme is selected. Ⓦ www.artsquarewinterfest.ru

● *Day becomes a White Night over St Petersburg and St Isaac's Cathedral*

History

For such an important city, St Petersburg has a relatively short history. Founded in 1703 by Peter the Great, it was built to both defend the nation from the constantly marauding Swedes and provide Russia with a forward-thinking port from which European ideals could breed and flourish.

Construction occurred rapidly as Peter lured skilled craftsmen with promises of land and brought thousands of indentured labourers to the construction sites. At the same time, Peter completely reformed the nobility, allowing honoured commoners to achieve status and wealth. Such valiant reforms caused the city to boom – so much so that, by the time of his death in 1725, the city boasted a population of 40,000.

Following the end of Peter's reign, the capital returned to Moscow for a brief period until the Empress Elizabeth came back in 1741 and commissioned the noted architect Rastrelli to create many of today's most celebrated buildings.

The peak of the city's decadence arrived when Catherine the Great acceded to the throne. She was a huge supporter of the Enlightenment and made efforts to liberalise Russia, until the French Revolution brought the idea of radicalism to Russian shores. This caused Catherine to turn away from the path of liberalism she had been following. Over the next century, St Petersburg grew until it became the fourth-largest city in Europe. Industrial opportunities abounded, yet the city suffered under the ineffectual leadership of rulers after Catherine.

In 1905, peacefully protesting workers were fired on by tsarist troops, resulting in months of uprising. Much to his chagrin, the tsar was forced to sign the October Manifesto, giving civil rights to the peasant classes.

World War I put a temporary freeze on revolutionary proceedings as the nation banded together to fight the German troops, even renaming the city Petrograd to give it a more Russian feel. Unfortunately for Tsar Nicolas II, however, war didn't put a stop to revolutionary thought, and the entire royal family was rounded up in 1917 and later assassinated.

From 1917 to 1921, the nation was rocked by civil war, resulting in the establishment of the one-party Communist system. The city was again renamed (this time Leningrad) to honour the death of the Communist party leader, Lenin.

World War II brought terrible hardship to the city as the Germans blockaded the metropolis for more than two years. A severe lack of food caused citizens to eat anything they could from wallpaper paste to leather belts – some even resorted to cannibalism.

After the war, Stalin returned to his old tricks, with little advancement of the economy occurring until the failure of the 1991 coup brought the breakup of the Soviet Union and eventual economic reforms. The city's old name was restored to the people. Today, St Petersburg is brighter than ever, following a massive regeneration scheme put in place to celebrate the city's 300th anniversary in 2003.

Lifestyle

A typical day for an average resident of St Petersburg varies greatly depending on what season it is. During the summer months, locals will spend as much time as they possibly can enjoying the outdoors. Evenings – which stay light for hours due to the city's northern latitude – see people drinking with friends at streetside cafés, strolling along the banks of the Neva river, and taking pleasure cruises on the murky water. This is, of course, after enjoying a trip to the country or to the beaches of the Gulf of Finland.

In winter, the weather plays havoc with any desire to step outside, with many locking themselves indoors or into cosy basement bars for as long as they can. You will note that there is a distinct personality change that occurs amongst locals as soon as the months of summer activity end.

Family life is key for Russians, usually overseen by a *babushka*-clad grandmother. These old ladies form the backbone of life: they often live with the younger generations, carry out many of the household chores, and queue patiently for supplies when necessary.

Politics remain a hot topic in this town that has changed names three times in the past hundred years. Residents have long memories, and know how seriously government can affect their daily lives. During your stay, you'll notice at least one protest of sorts – usually involving groups of elderly people demanding a return to the days of law and order. When capitalism arrived, St Petersburg's older population were very hard hit as guaranteed retirement incomes were thrown out of the window. Many have been forced to beg on the streets to supplement the meagre savings they scraped together over the years. Try not to get angry if you get approached more than once along Nevsky Prospekt.

КАЗАЧЬИ
БАНИ

ПАРИКМАХЕРСКАЯ
ВСЕ ВИДЫ
УСЛУГ
НИЗКИЕ ЦЕНЫ

○ Banyas – or bathhouses – are great for relaxing

Culture

In the land of Tchaikovsky, the Kirov Ballet and Dostoevsky, you don't have to look too hard to find a range of enjoyable offerings for those wanting to soak up the culture. A night at the theatre or ballet is a major event for locals and they dress up for the occasion. Tuxedoes and evening gowns are commonplace, even when it's not an opening night.

Tickets often sell out well in advance, so if you are arriving at a peak time you will either have to buy your tickets through your hotel concierge for a hefty fee, or reserve it in advance. If you're lucky, you can always try the box office of the venue you are hoping to attend or the central box office located at Nevsky Prospekt 42. Whatever you do, don't buy tickets from street sellers as they are often forgeries.

The most in-demand seats are always for performances at the world-renowned Mariinsky Theatre, especially for the Kirov Ballet. Opera at the Mariinsky is just as stunning, primarily due to the magic touch of the director Valery Gergiev. Russians tend to favour Italian and French language operas, so expect a lot of Puccini on the bill.

Classical music is supported with the same enthusiasm as your average Madonna concert and public performances are scheduled throughout the year to meet demand. The largest outdoor festival occurs during the Stars of the White Nights Festival in June; however, regular choral performances can also be found in the city's working Orthodox churches.

Despite the fact that this is the city that gave the world Chekhov, theatre is less well supported than other art forms.

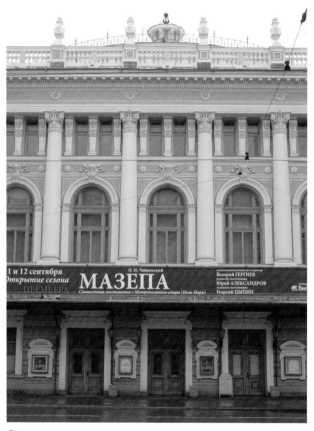

⬥ *The Mariinsky Theatre is a world-renowned venue*

Most performances are in Russian, meaning that visitors rarely step inside – but fans of drama will appreciate the staging techniques and acting quality.

Artistic possibilities aren't limited to adults. Children also appreciate local entertainment in the form of the puppet theatres and circuses that dot the city. If you have an aversion to animal acts, you might want to avoid the big top, but the puppet theatres are sure to please. You don't need a mastery of Russian to appreciate the performances, as the detail behind the creation of the puppets is more than enough to divert even the fussiest of little ones.

Finally, there are the museums. There are literally dozens of world-class galleries that could divert your attention for days. Admission charges can be high, but the number of exhibits warrants the steep entry fee. The top museums to put on your list include the Russian Museum, the Hermitage and the State Museum of the City of St Petersburg.

● *The waterways provide a different view of the city*

Shopping

Shopping in St Petersburg can challenge even the most patient, as many local retail staff continue to cling on to Communist, anti-capitalist notions. In many shops you will have to queue at least twice before walking out the door with your purchase – and you can pretty much forget about service with a smile. The variety of goods on offer is much better than it was a decade ago, as new generations embrace the world of international labels, but you still won't find shopping malls. During the summer months it might seem like a pleasant change to be outside visiting individual shops, but you'll be praying for a bit of climate-controlled capitalist happiness once the winter sets in.

For a one-stop souvenir shop, tourists flock to the market next to St Isaac's Cathedral. Here is where you will find a plethora of wares ranging from lacquerware to nesting dolls to Communist memorabilia. The prices are competitive due to the number of stallholders selling exactly the same thing, even if

USEFUL SHOPPING PHRASES

How much is...?
Сколько стоит?
skol-ka sto-it?

I'm a size...
Мой размер…
moy raz-myer

Can I try this on?
Можно это примерить?
mozh-na e-ta prim-ye-rit?

I'll take this one
Возму
vaz-mu

the quality does vary. Be on the look-out for military items that make great gifts for the men in your life – a nice change from the usual pair of socks, tie or novelty golf tees.

For true antiques, you'll have to pay top ruble. The best boutiques are found close to Nevsky Prospekt or in the Gallery Bolshaya Konyushennaya. Getting the antiques out of the country is ten times more difficult than saving up the money to pay for the items, as you will need an export licence from the Ministry of Culture. Most boutiques can take care of the paperwork – for a price.

Caviar is another popular purchase and you will be offered plenty of it by black-market dealers up and down Nevsky Prospekt. Don't fall for their sales patter as the types they sell are of much inferior quality and have been illegally obtained through poaching. Any caviar you buy should be in a sealed tin that has not been tampered with. The best varieties can be picked up at Yeliseevsky's. Note that you are limited to exporting a maximum of 250 g (8 oz) of black varieties at any one time.

Souvenir hunters can find Russian dolls of all designs and sizes

Eating & drinking

St Petersburg is truly a hit and miss town when it comes to dining out. For every memorable meal there will always be one you would prefer to forget. This is due to the fact that the transition from the years of Communist frugality has been a slow-moving process, with quality control and organic produce low on the list of priorities.

For locals, eating out is reserved only for rare occasions. As such, you will find that at most high- and middle-ranking establishments, you will be surrounded only by other tourists. This habit is slowly changing as the middle class gets more affluent – but even then it will be an uphill battle to convince residents that restaurants are more than just a luxury.

For a main course in a high-class eatery, expect to pay approximately R500. This price can soar, however, if you start ordering caviar or items that have to be shipped into the region. Budget-conscious travellers benefit from the limited funds of locals, as there are plenty of fast-food and worker canteens that dish up meals to the masses. While the quality is average at best, the opportunities to mix with everyday residents more than make up for the lack of flavour.

Reservations are rarely required at city restaurants unless they are brand new, have limited seating or are extremely luxurious. The only exception to this rule occurs during the White Nights festival, when the city is overrun with tourists and booking is essential.

Russians traditionally do not tip for service; however, it is always appreciated. In low- and mid-price establishments you won't be expected to do so. Five-star service should, however, receive about 10 per cent on top of the bill.

The old saying that breakfast is the most important meal of the day is heartily endorsed by Russians, with a typical morning meal packed with stodgy favourites such as curd cheese (*tvorog*), porridge (*kasha*) and pancakes (*bliny*). Ask nicely and you may even get some fruit compote to go with it.

The main meal of the day is always lunch, usually eaten between 13.00 and 16.00. Locals take their time over this meal, although restaurants are well aware that visitors prefer to eat a large meal at dinner and cater to this fact. Typical dishes boast peasant origins and make free use of ingredients such as cabbage, potatoes and dense, black bread.

A typical lunch begins with soup, usually cabbage or beetroot (*borscht*). In summer, chilled soups are also popular. Following this will be a meat dish of either pork or beef in sauce (usually mushroom). Alternatively, the meat may be formed into a form of ravioli known as *pelmeni* that is served in a light broth.

Ethnic influences drawn from across the Russian empire can also crop up during the main course in the form of Georgian kebabs or lightly-spiced Uzbek meats complete with pilau rice.

PRICE RATING
The price ratings given in this book indicate the approximate cost of a three-course meal for one person, excluding drinks.
£ up to R350   ££ R350–R850   £££ over R850

Unlike other Russian cities, St Petersburg has a tradition of serving fish and seafood, due to its proximity to the Gulf of Finland. The most common choices are herring, cod, salmon and sturgeon. Vegetables are not usually served with the main course and need to be ordered separately. Often, the only choice will be a combination of potatoes and/or tomatoes.

Dessert is not normally offered to Russians, despite the fact that locals adore ice cream. A typical street corner will always have an ice-cream stand, even in the depths of winter. As for alcohol, you can't beat the variety of vodka on sale in this country of dedicated drinkers. Vodka is usually served chilled and drunk in shot form followed very quickly by a morsel of food. Don't ever purchase vodka on the street: much of it is produced illegally and could include ingredients toxic to the average human being.

USEFUL DINING PHRASES

I'd like a table for two
Я бы хотел столик на две
ya bih khat-yel sto-lik na dvye

Could I have the bill please?
пожалуйста суёт?
pa-zhal-sta shot?

Waiter!
официант!
a-fit-sih-ant!

It is meat free?
Зто без мяса?
e-ta byez mya-sa?

Where is the toilet?
Где туалет?
g-dye too-a-lyet?

⬥ *The height of luxury: a cache of caviar*

Entertainment & nightlife

A little over a decade ago, nightlife in St Petersburg was limited to the number of things you could do after drinking a bottle of vodka. Times have changed and the city has now become one of the most decadent on the planet. Anything goes in this town (if you have the money), with an evening out potentially costing a hefty sum, depending on what you're after.

As in most Eastern European areas, the fall of Communism brought a sharp rise in the number of strip and 'gentlemen's' clubs. These entertainment spots are popular with both rich locals and visiting business types alike. Be warned that most of the women who work in these clubs are 'professionals', who may ask if you want to give them a hefty tip for services rendered later in the evening. No matter what they say or how often it is offered up, prostitution is illegal in Russia, and you are not advised to accept any propositions.

Another big trend is in gay clubs. Bars and nightspots catering to the gay community are exploding as heterosexual women find them much less oppressive than their straight counterparts. Gay clubs are starting to become more mixed as the Russian population slowly liberalises. It is wise, however, to be careful when entering or leaving a gay club, as homosexuality is still viewed by many as unnatural and attacks on gay people are common.

One weird quirk to remember about clubs in St Petersburg is that most work on a tab system. At the beginning of the evening you will be given a slip of paper. Each time you order a drink, hand the paper to the bartender and they will scrawl the

⬤ *Understatement is not the watchword at this St Petersburg restaurant*

amount on the tab. When you leave at the end of the evening, the cashier will add up the total and charge you for everything at once. Hold on to the tab very carefully as you will not be able to leave the club without it. Otherwise, you will have to pay a hefty bar fine amounting to a lot more than anything you might have ordered throughout the evening.

Trips to clubs and bars start late in this town, with venues getting going not much before midnight. Many a visitor has stumbled out of a happening hotspot after oodles of vodka to find themselves drunk in the middle of the day.

❶ The number of cases of tranquillisers being dropped into the drinks of tourists is on the increase, so if you do order drinks, be sure to keep your eye on them at all times. When travelling in a pair, always have one person guarding the refreshments. And if travelling alone, make sure you take your drink with you at all times if you are moving around. Never go back to a drink that has been unattended.

Finally, if the idea of dancing till dawn doesn't appeal, there are always the coffee shops. In this city formed by politics, coffee shops remain a popular place to debate the worries of the world among friends. The jolts of caffeine and scrumptious desserts ain't so bad either. Many chains remain open 24 hours, meaning you can debate with new friends and old until the wee hours of the morning.

Sport & relaxation

There's a reason why the Russians continue to dominate the Olympics – they absolutely love their sport. During the summer, locals squeeze every minute of sunshine out of the day in order to store the rays up to help get them through the long winter months. Swimming is a popular pastime and there are heaps of beaches to choose from. While many do dunk themselves in the Neva, the heavy pollution levels should make you think twice. The cleanest stretches of sand are on the shore west of Ozerki metro station or at the Gulf of Finland, which can be reached by going from Finland Station to Sestroretsk and then walking ten minutes through a nearby forest. Public pools are another option, though you will need a health certificate issued by the doctor in residence in order to give you access to facilities. If you are desperate to cool down, head to VMF located at Sredny pr 87 on Vasilevskiy Island.

Fitness centres are increasing in popularity, but you won't find equipment that matches even the most basic Western European sports centre. The truly determined should check out the Planet Fitness chain. There are six locations dotted throughout the city: try the branch at Kazanskaya Ulitsa 37 near the Sadovaya metro.

Finally, to relax, there is the ultimate Russian experience – the *banya*. A *banya* is like a sauna and is a regular meeting place for local groups of friends. Residents think nothing of dragging their closest confidants down to the *banya* to strip off, sweat, gossip and whip each other with birch twigs. It may sound bizarre, but the end result is extremely reviving. Facilities are usually single sex, with admission including the cost of sandals, sheet and towel rentals. Two of the best are:

Kruglye Bani ⓐ Ulitsa Karbysheva 29A. ① 550 0958
⊙ 08.00–21.00 Fri–Tues Ⓜ Metro: Ploshchad Muzhestva.

Mitninskaya Banya ⓐ Ulitsa Mitninskaya 17–19 ① 271 7119
⊙ 08.00–22.00 Fri–Tues Ⓜ Metro: Ploshchad Vosstaniya

⬤ *Ice hockey is a favourite in a sports-mad city*

Accommodation

Thanks to the celebrations of the city's 300th anniversary, the city got a much-needed injection of mid-priced hotel options following years of lack of choice. Until the arrival of these new three-star properties, visitors had a limited choice between five-star palaces, fleabag motels and shoddy Intourist hotels built during the years of Soviet austerity. Hostels have also been cropping up due to the newfound status of the city on the backpacker trail. High season lasts from May to September and hotel prices rise by as much as 30 per cent during this period. Add an 18 per cent VAT chargeable on all Russian hotel rooms, and things can get pretty expensive. When making a booking, be sure to check whether this price is included in the quoted rate. Also, when paying your final total, note that your bill will be quoted in US dollars or euros, but you will be expected to pay in rubles.

Reservations are imperative during the summer months, especially if you hope to stay during the White Nights festival. Your visa will demand the address of your hotel in order to

PRICE RATING
Hotels in Russia are graded according to a star system running from one star for a cheap guesthouse to five stars for a luxurious property with numerous facilities. The ratings in this book are as follows:
£ up to R2,500   **££** R2,500–R5,000   **£££** over R5,000
All prices are for a single night in a double or twin room.

receive approval, so you will need to book your stay before you arrive in the country anyway. When preparing to complete your visa application, ask your hotel for an 'invitation'. This is a necessary part of the process and most good locations should have no problem issuing you with one.

HOTELS

Nevsky Inn £ Clean rooms run efficiently by expat Brits. The modern kitchen can be used by residents. ⓐ Kirpichny Pereulok 2, flat 19 ⓣ 924 9805 Ⓝ Metro: Nevsky Prospekt

Hotel Mercury £–££ In its heyday, this was the address of choice for Communist party officials. While it no longer brings in the political elite, it retains a touch of grandeur despite the ultra-Soviet feel. ⓐ Tavricheskaya Ulitsa 39 ⓣ 325 6444 Ⓝ Metro: Chernyshevskaya

Austrian Yard Hotel ££ Four-room establishment for those looking for a comfortable, quiet place. ⓐ Furshtatskaya Ulitsa 45 ⓣ 579 8235 Ⓦ www.austrianyard.com Ⓝ Metro: Chernyshevskaya

Comfort Hotel ££ While the hotel is located on one of the coolest streets in town, its rooms are a little basic for the price you pay, but it's very convenient for the Hermitage and St Isaac's. ⓐ Bolshaya Morskaya Ulitsa 25 ⓣ 318 6700 Ⓦ www.comfort-hotel.spb.ru Ⓝ Metro: Nevsky Prospekt

Kazanskaya ££ Artists and bohemians love this elegantly appointed boutique property crammed with antiques. Despite the plethora of art and photography, rooms are delightfully modern in feel. ⓐ Kazanskaya Ulitsa 5, 3rd fl ⓣ 327 7466 ⓦ www.kazanskaya5.com ⓝ Metro: Nevsky Prospekt

Angleterre/Astoria £££ Sir Rocco Forte renovated this superb collection of two hotels in one. The Angleterre is the four-star property with chic décor and smallish rooms. The Astoria offers sumptuous interiors and stunning views of the square below. Guests have included Lenin and President Bush. Ah, the irony! Angleterre: ⓐ Bolshaya Morskaya Ulitsa 39 ⓣ 313 5112 ⓦ www.angleterrehotel.com ⓝ Metro: Nevsky Prospekt Astoria: ⓐ Bolshaya Morskaya Ulitsa 39 ⓣ 313 5757 ⓦ www.roccofortehotels.com ⓝ Metro: Nevsky Prospekt

Grand Hotel Europe £££ The location is perfect. The interiors top-notch. And the sense of history seeps through every marble and gilt-clad wall. If you have the cash, then there really is no other place to stay. ⓐ Mikhailovskaya Ulitsa 1/7 ⓣ 329 6000 ⓦ www.grandhoteleurope.com ⓝ Metro: Gostiniy Dvor

Renaissance St Petersburg Baltic Hotel £££ This property is the newest five-star in the city, and it lacks the atmosphere found in other, more historic, properties. Rooms are large and lavish and have superb views – but you can't help wishing you were staying at the Grand Hotel Europe or the Astoria instead. ⓐ Pochtamtskaya Ulitsa 4 ⓣ 380 4000 ⓦ www.renaissancehotels.com ⓝ Metro: Sadovaya

GUESTHOUSES AND B&BS

Guesthouse £ Simple, yet welcoming guesthouse with English-speaking staff. Located on a calm street just behind the Oktyabrsky Concert Hall ⓐ Grechesky Prospekt 13 ⓘ 271 3089 ⓦ www.ghspb.ru ⓝ Metro: Ploshchad Vosstaniya

B&B Nevsky Prospekt ££ Location is what makes this B&B so attractive. Staff speak English and guests can use the shared laundry and kitchen facilities. Prices are a little on the high side for what you get. Free airport transfers are included. ⓐ Nevsky Prospekt 11, apt 8 ⓘ 325 9398 ⓦ www.bnbrussia.com ⓝ Metro: Nevsky Prospekt

HOSTELS

Nord Hostel £ Freshly decorated dorm rooms and a convenient location smack-dab next to the Hermitage. Students even get free entry to the collection. Staff speak English and the shared kitchen facilities mean you can cook your meals to keep costs down. ⓐ Bolshaya Morskaya Ulitsa 10 ⓘ 571 0342 ⓦ www.nordhostel.com ⓝ Metro: Nevsky Prospekt

Puppet Hostel £ Less convenient than the Nord, the Puppet offers basic rooms with shared facilities. Guests receive free tickets to the Puppet Theatre next door. ⓐ Ul Nekrasova 12 ⓘ 272 5401 ⓦ www.hostel-puppet.ru ⓝ Metro: Mayakovskaya

---

▶ *Luxury and location make the Grand Hotel Europe the pick of the bunch*

THE BEST OF ST PETERSBURG

St Petersburg offers so much that your challenge will not be how to fill a weekend, but what you're going to have to miss. After one visit, you'll be sure to start budgeting for your next stay.

TOP 10 ATTRACTIONS

- **The Hermitage** The royal family's Winter Palace was transformed into the world's largest art gallery. The Impressionist collection alone is worth the cost of admission (see pages 71–3)

- **Peter & Paul Fortress** The oldest large-scale building in St Petersburg was built to defend against the Swedes – yet never saw any action (see pages 102–3)

- **Russian Museum** The finest Russian art available. A must-see for those wanting to expand their knowledge of Russian culture (see pages 87–9)

- **Peterhof** Peter the Great built this Russian palace to rival Versailles, and it certainly does (see pages 114–16)

- **St Isaac's Cathedral** Onion domes and sumptuous mosaics. This is what an Orthodox church should look like (see pages 63–4)

- **Sweating in a *banya*** Sit down, get hot, whip yourself with twigs – it's all in a day's relaxation (see pages 33–4)

- **Tsarskoe Selo** The favoured summer retreat of the royal family during the years of Catherine the Great – and it's easy to see why (see pages 118–20)

- **White Nights** Find out what happens when the sun always shines (see pages 13–14)

- **Nevsky Prospekt** Shop for caviar, step into the Grand Hotel or just watch the hordes go by (see pages 44–5)

- **Mariinsky Theatre** Ballet the way it was meant to be danced (see page 70)

▼ *The Hermitage is one of the city's unmissable sights*

HALF-DAY: ST PETERSBURG IN A HURRY

Head straight to the Hermitage, making sure to plot your route before you arrive. The Winter Palace is massive, so if you want to see the highlights, you'll have to do some planning if you only have a half-day.

1 DAY: TIME TO SEE A LITTLE MORE

Start your day at the souvenir market near St Isaac's Cathedral before popping into the church itself. Cross the Admiralty gardens to spend a few hours in the Hermitage. Continue along until you reach Dvortsovaya Ploshchad. Once you hit the canal, follow it to your right until you arrive at Nevsky Prospekt and follow the crowds as they meander along this main thoroughfare. End your day with a spot of caviar at the Grand Hotel Europe and feel like a tsar.

2–3 DAYS: SHORT CITY BREAK

Follow the plan suggested for a one-day trip and then get out of town to explore the wonders of Peterhof. It's an easy train or coach ride and there are plenty of tour operators who offer a full day package. If you have extra time, either plan a full day in the Hermitage or head over to the Russian Museum.

LONGER: ENJOYING ST PETERSBURG TO THE FULL

Divide the city into equal sections, making sure to give the Hermitage a full day of your time. Spend one day exploring the Peter & Paul Fortress and the sights on the Strelka at Vasilevsky Island. Budget two days for the sights of the city centre within the Fontanka, and then go beyond the canal for a day to take a

look at sights outside the downtown core. If you like, book a cruise along the Neva and then plan a couple of days exploring the historic royal palaces in the countryside.

▲ *Head for the Hermitage*

Something for nothing

Unfortunately for visitors, even the most minor of museums charges an admission fee. This is due to the fact that most artistic and cultural institutions receive absolutely no other financial assistance. Your best bet if you're on a budget is to admire the architecture and history of the city from the street. A lack of money for renovations means that exterior views are often more impressive than the interiors anyway.

A stroll through city squares brings you into contact with some of the most important locations in St Petersburg, including Dvortsovaya Ploshchad, considered by most to be the square that launched the revolution of 1905, for it was here where tsarist troops fired on peaceful workers protesting the harsh regime.

Another favoured public area is the Summer Gardens – once the private gardens of Peter the Great. This path-filled green space nestles on the banks of the Neva river and boasts a number of lime trees that provide shade during the summer months.

A weekend walk along Nevsky Prospekt has long been the height of fashion for locals, whether they are up for a shop or not. This elegant boulevard runs 4.5 km (nearly 3 miles) in length and measures up to 60 m (197 ft) across in some places. Street life is varied and can include encounters with beggars, *babushka*-clad women, fur-clad *nouveaux riches* and gypsies. During June, when the sun stays up for most of the day, sidewalk traffic can buzz at even the earliest hours as locals take advantage of the often vodka-soaked summer months.

In an effort to reintroduce religion to the masses, churches and synagogues are often open to the public free of charge, although the grandest cathedrals remain both secular and expensive. Inside free places of worship you will usually find austere interiors, occasional art exhibits and displays describing the building's history. Notable freebie attractions include the Kazan Cathedral, Grand Choral Synagogue, Church of St John of Kronstadt, Preobrazhenskiy Church and Vladimirskiy Cathedral.

🔺 *Stroll along Nevsky Prospekt and soak up the atmosphere*

When it rains

St Petersburg is not a city blessed with the best of weather. When it rains, it pours – and when it snows, it can pummel the city with massive banks of the white stuff. During inclement periods, the most logical place to go to is the Hermitage. The massive collection could take the average visitor days to explore, meaning that even the most art-phobic of tourists could kill a few hours within its glorious walls.

The Russian Museum is another good place to head for when the weather gets tough, packed with its impressive collections of Russian art, including some fabulous examples of iconography.

If you would prefer something a little less museum-orientated, and you have some cash to spare, then what better than a little caviar tasting? The Caviar Bar at the Grand Hotel Europe is the place to do it, but you'll have to pay through the nose for the privilege. Alternatively, make a quick dash through the rain to Yeliseevsky's, a food hall once mentioned in the pages of *Anna Karenina*. This *style moderne* masterpiece is heaven for foodies, and you can kill an hour just by staring at the content in the refrigerators alone. An even larger shopping emporium is Gostiny Dvor, a department store that has been the one-stop shop for locals since the 19th century. While the wares aren't all that impressive these days, the size alone should keep you occupied and out of the wet.

Finally, there are the theatres. If you strike it lucky, you can pick up tickets to see the Kirov in performance. Otherwise, take the kids to the Bolshoy Puppet Theatre where tots and teens will be entranced by the beautifully constructed puppets on

display. There are 16 plays geared for children in the repertoire and two for adults, meaning that return visits can be programmed into your stay. A godsend for parents looking to keep kids amused.

🔺 *Travel by metro if the weather takes a turn for the worse*

On arrival

ARRIVING
By air

Most of those travelling by air to St Petersburg will arrive at Pulkovo-2 International Airport. Only two airlines serve the city non-stop from the United Kingdom: Aeroflot and British Airways. Aeroflot has a bad reputation in terms of both service and safety, but a major revamp aims to alter perceptions. International services tend to be better than domestic.

Pulkovo-2 is located 17 km (10½ miles) south of the city and looks a lot better following a much-needed renovation in 2003. Domestic services depart from and arrive at Pulkovo-1 airport a few kilometres away.

To get to the city centre from Pulkovo, take the 13 or K3 city bus and connect to the Moskovskaya metro station. Buses run every 15 minutes. Another option is to take a *marshrutka*, an unlicensed minibus taxi that is used most commonly by locals. Simply flag one down and take it to the city centre or nearest metro station by telling the driver your destination. Taxis are extraordinarily expensive, costing as much as £50 one way. Better rates can be organised by your hotel prior to your arrival.

Airport information
Pulkovo Airport ❶ 104 3444.

Airline
Aeroflot ❶ 020 7409 2779 ❢ www.aeroflot.com
British Airways ❶ 0870 850 9850 ❢ www.ba.com

By rail

There are five main rail stations that serve the city, each going to destinations in a different region. Local trains arrive at and depart from Baltiysky station. Use this station should you plan a visit to Oranienbaum. Moscow station is the point of call for trains to – you guessed it – Moscow. Vitebsk station deals with trains departing and arriving from Eastern Europe, including Poland, Belarus, the Czech Republic, the Baltics, Kaliningrad and Hungary. For Finland and northern Russia you will use Ladozhsky station, while (confusingly) Finland station is used for suburban trains going towards Vyborg.

By road

St Petersburg is an extremely difficult city to drive in. Street signs are in Cyrillic and city drivers are notoriously chaotic. If you do decide to drive to St Petersburg, remember that left turns are illegal and that overtaking on the inside is commonplace.

⬥ *The Aeroflot terminal at Pulkovo-2 International*

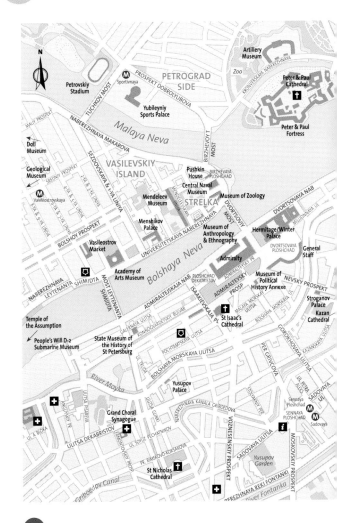

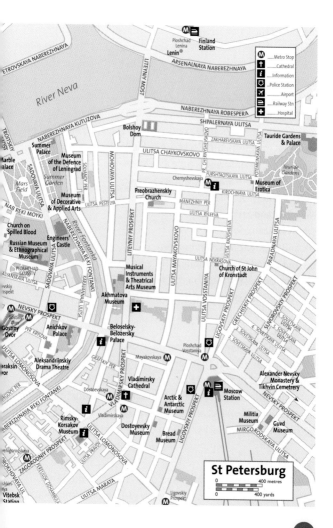

Ploshchad Lenina
Finland Station
Lenin
ARSENALNAYA NABEREZHNAYA

ETROVSKAYA NABEREZHNAYA

River Neva

NABEREZHNAYA ROBESPERA

SHPALERNAYA ULITSA

Bolshoy Dom

ZAKHAREVSKAYA ULITSA

Tauride Gardens & Palace

NABEREZHNAYA KUTUZOVA

Summer Palace

Museum of the Defence of Leningrad

ULITSA CHAYKOVSKOVO

Marble Palace

Mars Field

Summer Garden

Museum of Decorative & Applied Arts

FURSHTAOTSKAYA ULITSA

Chernyshevskaya

ULITSA PESTELYA

Preobrazhenskiy Church

MANEZHNIY PER

KIROCHNAYA ULITSA

Museum of Erotica

Church on Spilled Blood

ULITSA RYLEEVA

Russian Museum & Ethnographical Museum

Engineers' Castle

ULITSA NEKRASOVA

Church of St John of Kronstadt

Musical Instruments & Theatrical Arts Museum

Akhmatova Museum

Gostiny Dvor
NEVSKY PROSPEKT

Anichkov Palace

Beloselsky-Belozersky Palace

Ploshchad Vosstaniya

Aleksandriinskiy Drama Theatre

GRAFSKIY PER

Mayakovskaya

Alexander Nevsky Monastery & Tikhvin Cemetery

Vladimirsky Cathedral

Dostoevskaya

Arctic & Antarctic Museum

NEVSKY PROSPEKT

Rimsky-Korsakov Museum

Vladimirskaya

Dostoevsky Museum

Bread Museum

Moscow Station

Militia Museum

Guvd Museum

MIRGORODSKAYA ULITSA

ZAGORODNIY PROSPEKT

ULITSA MARATA

Vitebsk Station

St Petersburg

0 — 400 metres
0 — 400 yards

Legend:
- Ⓜ ......Metro Stop
- ......Cathedral
- ⓘ ......Information
- ......Police Station
- ......Airport
- ......Railway Stn
- ✚ ......Hospital

If arriving via Finland, follow the M-10 directly to the city centre. From the Baltics, take the M-20 and change onto the M-10 when you reach the city outskirts.

TIME DIFFERENCES

St Petersburg's clocks follow Moscow Standard Time (MST), which is three hours ahead of GMT. During Daylight Saving Time (end Mar–end Oct), the clocks are put ahead one hour. In St Petersburg, at 12.00 noon, time elsewhere is as follows:

Australia Eastern Standard Time 19.00, Central Standard Time 18.30, Western Standard Time 17.00

New Zealand 21.00

South Africa 11.00

UK and Republic of Ireland 09.00

US and Canada Newfoundland Time 05.30, Atlantic Canada Time 05.00, Eastern Standard Time 04.00, Central Time 03.00, Mountain Time 02.00, Pacific Time 01.00, Alaska 24.00

FINDING YOUR FEET

St Petersburg's centre is compact and walkable. There are, however, many sights that lie outside the core that can be difficult to reach. For travel between districts, the metro system gets you close to most corners of the city. Unfortunately, it doesn't go everywhere, and you may have a bit of a walk once you reach the stop closest to your destination.

ORIENTATION

Due to the number of canals and rivers that cut through St Petersburg, a grid system never really caught on in this relatively

new Russian city. The city centre is considered the middle of the city, bordered to the north by the Neva and to the south by the Fontanka. Outside of the Fontanka, the city continues until it reaches the Obvodniy Canal, which effectively cuts the city centre peninsula from the mainland. To the west of the city centre and linked by a bridge is Vasilevskiy Island. This island creates a fork for the Neva river, which flows around it into the Gulf of Finland. Continue north across another bridge from Vasilevskiy Island and you reach Petrograd Side, a cluster of delta islands, and the location where Peter the Great first broke ground to build the city. East of the city centre and across the Neva river is what is known as Vyborg Side, the section of the city that failed to capture the eye of Peter the Great and holds few sights as a result.

GETTING AROUND

St Petersburg can be navigated by metro, tram and bus. Trams are old, inefficient, slow and prone to derailment. While they look cute, few locals take them – and for good reason. Buses are crowded and slow. Take them only if you are trying to get to

IF YOU GET LOST, TRY ...

Do you speak English?
Вы говорите по-английски?
vih ga-va-rit-ye pa-ang-li-ski?

Where is...?
Где...?
g-dye...?

Could you show me on the map?
Покажите мне, пожалуйста на карте?
pa-ka-zhih-tye mnye pa-zhal-sta na kart-ye?

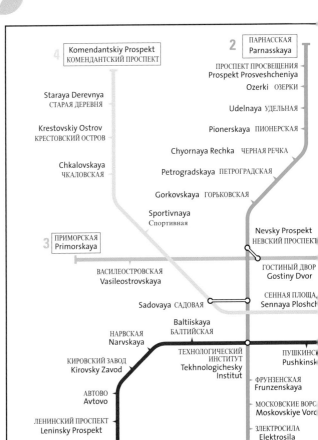

4 Komendantskiy Prospekt
КОМЕНДАНТСКИЙ ПРОСПЕКТ

2 ПАРНАССКАЯ
Parnasskaya

ПРОСПЕКТ ПРОСВЕЩЕНИЯ
Prospekt Prosveshcheniya

Ozerki ОЗЕРКИ

Staraya Derevnya
СТАРАЯ ДЕРЕВНЯ

Udelnaya УДЕЛЬНАЯ

Krestovskiy Ostrov
КРЕСТОВСКИЙ ОСТРОВ

Pionerskaya ПИОНЕРСКАЯ

Chyornaya Rechka ЧЕРНАЯ РЕЧКА

Chkalovskaya
ЧКАЛОВСКАЯ

Petrogradskaya ПЕТРОГРАДСКАЯ

Gorkovskaya ГОРЬКОВСКАЯ

Sportivnaya
Спортивная

Nevsky Prospekt
НЕВСКИЙ ПРОСПЕКТ

3 ПРИМОРСКАЯ
Primorskaya

ГОСТИНЫЙ ДВОР
Gostiny Dvor

ВАСИЛЕОСТРОВСКАЯ
Vasileostrovskaya

СЕННАЯ ПЛОЩА
Sennaya Ploshch

Sadovaya САДОВАЯ

Baltiiskaya
БАЛТИЙСКАЯ

НАРВСКАЯ
Narvskaya

ТЕХНОЛОГИЧЕСКИЙ
ИНСТИТУТ
Tekhnologichesky
Institut

ПУШКИНС
Pushkinsk

КИРОВСКИЙ ЗАВОД
Kirovskiy Zavod

ФРУНЗЕНСКАЯ
Frunzenskaya

АВТОВО
Avtovo

МОСКОВСКИЕ ВОРС
Moskovskiye Voro

ЛЕНИНСКИЙ ПРОСПЕКТ
Leninsky Prospekt

ЭЛЕКТРОСИЛА
Elektrosila

ПАРК ПОБЕДЫ
Park Pobedy

ПРОСПЕКТ ВЕТЕРАНОВ **1**
Prospekt Veteranov

МОСКОВСКАЯ
Moskovskaya

ЗВЕЗДНАЯ
Zvezdnaya

КУПЧИНО **2**
Kupchino

ДЕВЯТКИНО
Devyatkino **1**

ГРАЖДАНСКИЙ ПРОСПЕКТ Grazhdansky Prospekt

АКАДЕМИЧЕСКАЯ Akademicheskaya

ПОЛИТЕХНИЧЕСКАЯ Politekhnicheskaya

ПЛОЩАДЬ МУЖЕСТВА Ploshchad Muzhestva

ЛЕСНАЯ Lesnaya

ВЫБОРГСКАЯ Vyborgskaya

ПЛОЩАДЬ ЛЕНИНА Ploshchad Lenina

ЧЕРНЫШЕВСКАЯ Chernyshevskaya

ПЛОЩАДЬ ВОССТАНИЯ Ploshchad Vosstaniya

ayakovskaya
МАЯКОВСКАЯ

Dostoyevskaya
ДОСТОЕВСКАЯ

Ploshchad Aleksandra Nevskovo
ПЛОЩАДЬ АЛЕКСАНДРА НЕВСКОГО

ВЛАДИМИРСКАЯ
Vladimirskaya

ЛИГОВСКИЙ
ПРОСПЕКТ
Ligovsky
Prospekt

НОВОЧЕРКАССКАЯ
Novocherkasskaya

ЕЛИЗАРОВСКАЯ
Yelizarovskaya

ЛОМОНОСОВСКАЯ
Lomonosovskaya

ЛАДОЖСКАЯ
Ladozhskaya

ПРОЛЕТАРСКАЯ
Proletarskaya

ПРОСПЕКТ БОЛЬШЕВИКОВ
Prospekt Bolshevikov

ОБУХОВО
Obukhovo

РЫБАЦКОЕ
3 Rybatskoye

УЛИЦА ДЫБЕНКО
Ulitsa Dybenko **4**

○ ⊂⊃ Interchange with other lines

ДЕВЯТКИНО
Devyatkino **1** Terminating station
& route number

hard-to-reach locations. Your best bets are *marshrutkas*, which are privately run minibuses flagged down on the street by locals. Tell the driver what direction you are going in – and if they're going that way, then get on board. Fares average around R14. Alternatively, take the metro. Convenient if you want to get to the suburbs, it fails somewhat in the city centre as it only offers three stations within this tourist-happy district. The flat fare for a single trip is R8 or R66 for a week-long pass valid for 10 journeys. Licensed taxis are a complete rip-off and should only be ordered through your hotel.

CAR HIRE

Unless you are planning drives out to explore the countryside and the royal palaces or points further afield, you won't need to hire a car. In the event that you do decide to get some wheels, be warned that Russian drivers can be very unpredictable – many don't have a licence (or have obtained it on the black market). Major thoroughfares got a lot better following celebrations of the city's 300th anniversary in 2003, but side streets continue to be riddled with potholes. Rates are usually on the expensive side due to the fact that city driving and car thefts make insurance premiums high. The minimum age for renting an economy car is 21.

Europcar ⓐ Nab. Reki Fontanki 38 ⓣ 380 1662
ⓦ www.europcar.ru ⓜ Metro: Gostiniy Dvor
Hertz ⓐ Pulkovo Airport Terminal 2 ⓣ 326 4505
ⓦ www.hertz.spb.ru

● *Ancient treasures in the Museum of Anthropology & Ethnology*

The city centre

The historic heart of St Petersburg is bounded by the Neva river to the north and the Fontanka to the south. This is the location for the finest shops and a range of historic attractions. A stroll along the Nevsky Prospekt is a must. Be sure to fortify yourself with some caviar from Yeliseevsky's for the journey!

SIGHTS & ATTRACTIONS

Admiralty
Site of the former headquarters of the Russian Navy, this military naval college is one of the city's most well-known landmarks. Closed to the public, it is worth visiting to admire its elegant exterior and gardens.
ⓐ Admiralteysky Prospekt 1 ① No phone ⓒ Closed to the public
Ⓜ Metro: Nevsky Prospekt

Anichkov Palace
The second-largest palace in the city was once given as a gift to Potemkin by Catherine the Great. A huge building, it is now used as an after-school club for over 10,000 children. As a result, much of the building is off limits to casual visitors.
ⓐ Nevsky Prospekt ① 310 8433 ⓒ 10.00–17.00 Mon–Fri Ⓜ Metro: Gostiny Dvor

Church on Spilled Blood
Built in 1881 to commemorate the assassination of Tsar Alexander II, this place of worship was intended to act as a

location where the nobility could privately mourn the leader's death. After the revolutionaries came to power, its doors were opened to the public. A massive restoration returned the church to its former state of glory in 1997.

ⓐ Konyushannaya Ploshchad ⓣ 315 1636 ⓒ 11.00–18.00 Thur–Tues; admission charge ⓜ Metro: Nevsky Prospekt

Dvortsovaya Ploshchad (Palace Square)

When tsarist troops fired on workers protesting in this square back in 1905, it sparked a revolution that eventually resulted in the storming of the Winter Palace 12 years later and the introduction of Communism. Considered the heart of the city,

ⓐ *Palace Square lies at the heart of the city*

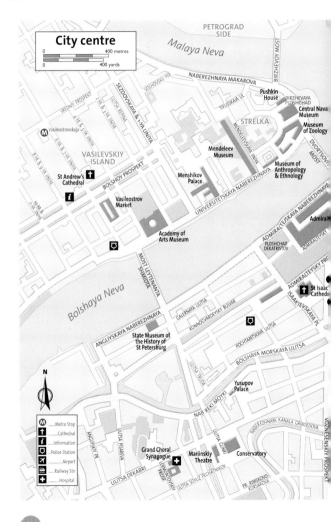

City centre

0 ——————— 400 metres
0 ——————— 400 yards

PETROGRAD SIDE

Malaya Neva

BIRZHEVOY MOST

NABEREZHNAYA MAKAROVA

SREDNIY PROSPEKT

SEZDOVSKAJA & 3.YA LINIYA

ULITSA REPINA

VOLHOVSKIJ PR.

TIFLISSKAA UL.

Pushkin House

BIRZHEVAYA PLOSHCHAD

Central Nava Museum

STRELKA

Museum of Zoology

Vasileostrovskaja

6YA & 7.YA LINIYA

8.YA & 9.YA LINIYA

MENDELEEVSKAYA LINIYA

DVORISOV.

VASILEVSKIY ISLAND

Mendeleev Museum

Museum of Anthropology & Ethnology

MOST

St Andrew's Cathedral

BOLSHOY PROSPEKT

Menshikov Palace

10.YA & 11.YA LINIYA

UNIVERSITETSKAYA NABEREZHNAYA

Vasileostrov Market

ADMIRALTEYSKAYA NABEREZHNAYA

Admiral

Academy of Arts Museum

MOST LEYTENANTA SHMIDTA

PLOSHCHAD DEKABRISTOV

ADMIRALTEYSKIY

Bolshaya Neva

CALERNAYA ULITSA

KONNOGVARDEYSKIY BULVAR

POCHTAMTSKAYA ULITSA

ADMIRALTEYSKIY PRO

St Isaac Cathedral

ISAAKIEVSKAYA PL.

ANGLIYSKAYA NABEREZHNAYA

State Museum of the History of St Petersburg

POCHTAMTSKAYA ULITSA

BOLSHAYA MORSKAYA ULITSA

ULITSA TRUDA

N

ULITSA GLINKI

Yusupov Palace

NAB. REKI MOYKI

NABEREZHNAYA KANALA GRIBOEDOVA

VOZNESENSKIY PROSPEKT

ANGLIISKIY PR.

ULITSA PISAREVA

LERMONTOVSKIY PROSP.

Grand Choral Synagogue

Mariinskiy Theatre

Conservatory

ULITSA DEKABRI

ULITSA SOYUZ PECHATNIKOV

PR. RIMSKOVO-KORSAKOVA

Ⓜ	Metro Stop
✝	Cathedral
ℹ	Information
⊚	Police Station
✈	Airport
🚉	Railway Stn
✚	Hospital

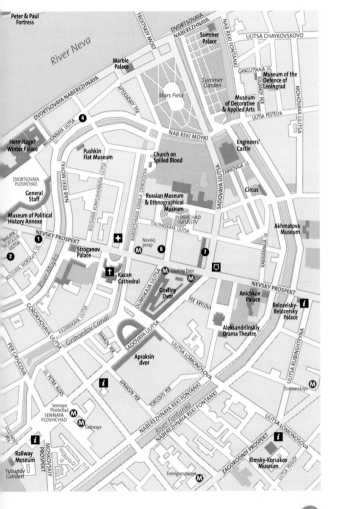

Peter & Paul
Fortress

River Neva

TROITSKIY MOST

DVORTSOVAYA
NABEREZHNAYA

NAB REKI FONTANKI

ULITSA CHAYKOVSKOVO

Summer
Palace

Marble
Palace

DVORTSOVAYA NABEREZHNAYA

APTEKARSKY PER

Mars Field

Summer
Garden

GANGUTSKAJA UL

SOLJANY PER

Museum of the
Defence of
Leningrad

MILJONNAYA ULITSA

Museum
of Decorative
& Applied Arts

MOHOVAYA ULITSA

ULITSA PESTELYA

NAB REKI MOYKI

Hermitage/
Winter Palace

Pushkin
Flat Museum

Church on
Spilled Blood

Engineers'
Castle

DVORTSOVAYA
PLOSHCHAD

General
Staff

NAB REKI MOYKI

BOLSHAIA KONUSHENNAYA ULITSA

NABEREZHNAYA KANALA GRIBOEDOVA

Russian Museum
& Ethnographical
Museum

SADOVAYA ULITSA

ZAMKOVAIA UL

Circus

Museum of Political
History Annexe

PLOSHCHAD
ISKUSSTV

ITALYANSKAIA ULITSA

Akhmatova
Museum

MALAYA
MORSKAYA
ULITSA

NEVSKY PROSPEKT

Nevskij
prosp

KARAVANNAJA UL

BOLSHAYA MORSKAYA UL

Stroganov
Palace

Kazan
Cathedral

Gostiny Dvor

NEVSKY PROSPEKT

River Moyka

Gostiny
Dvor

DUMSKAIA ULITSA

PER KRYLOVA

Anichkov
Palace

Beloselsky-
Belozersky
Palace

GOROHOVAIA ULITSA

KAZANSKAIA UL

Griboedov Canal

BANKOV PER

SADOVAYA ULITSA

Aleksandriinskiy
Drama Theatre

ULITSA RUBINSHTEINA

PER GRIVCOVIA

UL PETRA ALEKS

Apraksin
dvor

ULITSA LOMONOSOVA

NABEREZHNAYA REKI FONTANKI

APRAKSIN PER

TOKGOVY PER

River Fontanka

Dostoevskaya

Sennaya
Ploshchad

SENNAYA
PLOSHCHAD

Sadovaya

NABEREZHNAYA REKI FONTANKI

STOLIARNY

MOSKOVSKIY PROSPEKT

Railway
Museum

Yusupov
Garden

ZAGORODNIY PROSPEKT

ULITSA LOMONOSOVA

UL PRJAD

Rimsky-Korsakov
Museum

Evenigorodskaya

it is packed with examples of grandeur past and present.
🅐 Dvortsovaya Ploshchad 🕐 No phone 🕒 24 hrs Ⓜ Metro: Nevsky Prospekt

Engineers' Castle

Tsar Paul built this medieval-looking structure in place of the wooden castle where he was born. He spent only 40 days within the walls before being murdered by conspirators. It is now a branch of the Russian Museum and displays portraits of the royal families and leading local figures.
🅐 Sadovaya Ulitsa 2 🕐 313 4173 Ⓦ www.rusmuseum.ru 🕒 10.00–18.00 Wed–Sun, 10.00–17.00 Mon Ⓜ Metro: Gostiny Dvor

Grand Choral Synagogue

St Petersburg once boasted a large Jewish population and this synagogue was the focal point of the community. The building was completely renovated in 2003. Men and women should bring something to cover their heads if they want to enter.
🅐 Lermontovskiy Prospekt 2 🕐 114 1153 🕒 (service) 10.00 Sat Ⓜ Metro: Sadovaya.

Kazan Cathedral

Tsar Paul had a dream to unite Catholicism and Orthodoxy – and this church was intended to be the main cathedral of the new religion. Paul was assassinated shortly after he commissioned the structure, yet it remains intriguing due to its unique look – modelled on St Peter's in Rome.
🅐 Kazansky Sobor 🕐 311 4826 Ⓦ www.kazansky.ru 🕒 11.00–19.00 Ⓜ Metro: Nevsky Prospekt

Marble Palace

Thirty-six kinds of marble were used to construct this fascinating palace, now used as a modern art gallery by the Russian Museum.

ⓐ Millionnaya Ulitsa 5 ⓣ 312 9196 ⓛ 10.00–17.00 Wed–Mon; admission charge ⓜ Metro: Nevsky Prospekt

Mars Field

Originally intended as a military parade ground when it was laid out by Tsar Alexander I, today it holds an eternal flame in honour of those who died during the 1917 Revolution.

ⓐ Marovo Polye ⓣ No phone ⓛ 24 hrs ⓜ Metro: Nevsky Prospekt

Ploshchad Dekabristov

This graceful square is best known for its statue of Peter the Great, known as the *Bronze Horseman*. A symbol of the city, it depicts the tsar on a horse as it rears above the snake of treason. Many feel it was commissioned by Catherine the Great to emphasise her philosophical link with the monarch due to her lack of a hereditary connection to the Russian throne.

ⓐ Ploshchad Dekabristov ⓣ No phone ⓛ 24 hrs
ⓜ Metro: Sadovaya

St Isaac's Cathedral

Other than the Hermitage, St Isaac's Cathedral is probably the most recognisable building in St Petersburg. Built in 1818, it is one of the largest domed buildings in the world and boasts an interior packed with stunning mosaics and ceiling paintings. The dome is covered by over 100 kg (220 lb) of gold leaf; it is

worth climbing the 262 steps to get amazing views over the city.
 Isaakievskaya Ploshchad ☎ 315 9732 ⓦ www.cathedral.ru
🕐 11.00–18.00 Thur–Tues; admission charge Ⓜ Metro: Sadovaya

Stroganov Palace

Elegant baroque palace built for the Stroganov family by
Rastrelli in 1753. Avoid the tacky waxwork museum inside.
ⓐ Nevsky Prospekt 17 ☎ 314 6424 🕐 10.00–18.00 Wed–Sun,
10.00–17.00 Mon; admission charge Ⓜ Metro: Nevsky Prospekt

Summer Palace & Garden

The palace in the Summer Garden grounds is tiny compared to
other locations lived in by the royal family. The gardens – once
Peter the Great's private retreat – are now a popular place for a
stroll, with hundreds of lime trees shading the paths.
ⓐ Muzey Letny Dvorets Petra 1 ☎ 314 0456 🕐 Palace: 10.00–17.00
Wed–Mon, May–Oct; Gardens: 09.00–22.00 May–Oct,
10.00–18.00 Nov–mid-Apr. Prospekt Gardens closed for last
two weeks of April; admission charge for palace only Ⓜ Metro:
Gostiny Dvor

Yusopov Palace

This palace is probably the finest in the city and once served as
the home to the great Yusopov family. While the well-preserved
19th-century interiors should be attraction enough, it is because
of its place in history as the location where Rasputin was
murdered that most visitors enter its doors.
ⓐ Nab Reki Moyki 94 ☎ 314 9883 🕐 11.00–17.00; admission
charge Ⓜ Metro: Sadovaya

🔺 *The Summer Palace & Garden*

CULTURE

Museum of Political History Annexe

Once home to the founder of the KGB, Felix Dzerzhinsky, this museum now holds exhibits detailing the history of police repression in Russia. Russian-language only.

ⓐ Admiralteysky Prospekt 6 ⓣ 312 2742 ⓛ 10.00–18.00 Mon–Fri; admission charge ⓜ Metro: Nevsky Prospekt

Pushkin Flat-Museum

The last home of the famed poet has been recreated to look exactly as it did on the day he died following a duel with a French nobleman in 1837. English tours must be arranged in advance.

ⓐ Nab. Reki Moyki 12 ⓣ 311 3531 ⓛ 10.30–18.00 Wed–Sun; admission charge ⓜ Metro: Nevsky Prospekt

State Museum of the History of St Petersburg

Excellent museum looking at the history of the city with particular focus on the 20th century.

ⓐ Angliyskaya Naberezhnaya 44 ⓣ 571 7544 ⓛ 11.00–17.00 Thur–Tues; admission charge ⓜ Metro: Sadovaya

RETAIL THERAPY

Shopping streets & markets

Gostiny Dvor This department store is the oldest in St Petersburg. Built in the mid-18th century, it has been a way of life for locals ever since it opened its doors. The articles for sale

aren't very inspiring, but the building is more than a draw in itself. ⓐ Nevsky Prospekt 35 ⓣ 110 5200 ⓦ www.gostinydvor.ru ⓛ 10.00–22.00 Ⓝ Metro: Gostiny Dvor

Lomosov One of Europe's oldest porcelain manufacturers, it has a showroom that befits the quality of its over 500 catalogue items. Go and be dazzled (or at least dazzle your table). ⓐ Grand Hotel Europe, Mikhailovskaya Ulitsa 1–7 ⓣ 329 6000 ⓛ 10.00–22.00 Ⓝ Metro: Gostiny Dvor

Vernissazh Market For souvenirs and kitsch, you can't get better than this market steps away from St Isaac's Cathedral. Pick up

▲ Waterways and bridges span the city

lacquerware, nesting dolls and military 'antiques'. Nab. Kanala Griboedova ● 08.00–21.00 ● Metro: Nevsky Prospekt

Yeliseevsky Russia's answer to the Harrods' food hall is this exquisite culinary masterpiece that is even referred to in the pages of *Anna Karenina*. It isn't the cheapest place to pick up caviar in the city, but it is certainly the best in terms of quality. ● Nevsky Prospekt 56 ● Phone unlisted ● 10.00–21.00 ● Metro: Gostiny Dvor

TAKING A BREAK

Idealnaya Chashka £ ❶ Russia's answer to Starbucks can be found on corners throughout the city, but this branch is one of the biggest and buzziest. ● Nevsky Prospekt 15 ● 320 6489 ● 08.00–23.00 ● Metro: Nevsky Prospekt

AFTER DARK

Restaurants
Dinastiya £ ❷ Simple, Russian, family-made fare. Great for local specialities on a budget. ● Gorokhovaya Ulitsa 11 ● 315 0754 ● 12.00–23.00 ● Metro: Nevsky Prospekt

Tandoor £ ❸ The oldest Indian restaurant in town may not offer anything too spicy, but it's a godsend for vegetarians who suffer in this nation of meat-worshippers. ● Voznesenskiy Prospekt 2 ● 312 3886 ● 12.00–23.00 ● Metro: Nevsky Prospekt

Kalif ££ ❹ This is the place to get Uzbek cuisine dished up with flair. Vegetarians will appreciate the extensive salad selection. Live music and belly dancing offered during the evening. ⓐ Millionnaya Ulitsa 21/6 ⓣ 312 2265 ⓛ 12.00–24.00 Ⓜ Metro: Nevsky Prospekt

Caviar Bar £££ ❺ For those with a massive expense account, the caviar bar is the place to go. Here you will be served chilled vodka, buckets of the finest sturgeon eggs and champagne galore. Prepare to walk away much poorer than when you arrived. ⓐ Grand Hotel Europe, Mikhailovskaya Ulitsa 1–7 ⓣ 329 6000 ⓛ 17.00–23.00 Ⓜ Metro: Nevsky Prospekt

Onegin £££ ❻ St Petersburg's most exclusive dining spot is this *nouveau riche* eatery packed to the gills with chandeliers and gold gilt. The food is just as rich as the décor and is deservedly acclaimed. ⓐ Sadovaya Ulitsa 11 ⓣ 571 8384 ⓦ www.oneginspb.com ⓛ 17.00–02.00 Ⓜ Metro: Gostiny Dvor

Bars, clubs & discos

Greshniki The city's premier gay venue is a magnet for both the pink community and their friends. Music tends to be on the trashy side. ⓐ Nab. Kanala Griboedova 29 ⓣ 318 4291 ⓛ Hours vary Ⓜ Metro: Gostiny Dvor

Opium For decent, Western-friendly music and an in-crowd of the city's cool crowd, go to Opium. Make sure you dress up, though, as the door policy is very choosy. ⓐ Sadovaya Ulitsa 12 ⓣ 312 0148 ⓛ Hours vary Ⓜ Metro: Gostiny Dvor

Cinema & theatre
Mariinsky Theatre

Book well in advance for tickets to any of the performances at this stunning ballet and opera house, home to the Kirov Ballet. Unlike at other theatres, suits and evening gowns are *de rigueur*. Teatralnaya Ploshchad 326 4141 www.mariinsky.ru (box office): 11.00–19.00 Metro: Sadovaya

Pushkin Theatre

While performances at this theatre often vary in terms of quality, its claim to fame is as the location where Chekhov's *Cherry Orchard* premiered over a century ago to critical condemnation. Ploshchad Ostrovskogo 2 110 4103 Box-office hours vary according to performance schedule Metro: Gostiny Dvor

St Petersburg State Circus Visit the circus for clowns, acrobats and high-wire acts galore. It is one to avoid, though, if you hate trained animal routines, as the non-human performers can look a little worse for wear. Nab. Reki Fontanki 3 314 8478 Box-office hours vary according to performance schedule Metro: Gostiny Dvor

Shostakovich Philharmonia The home of the St Petersburg Philharmonic Orchestra under the direction of much-lauded maestro Yuri Temirkanov. Tickets sell out fast, so you will need to book ahead. Mikhailovskaya Ulitsa 2 110 4257 www.philharmonia.spb.ru Metro: Nevsky Prospekt

THE HERMITAGE

A visitor could spend days in the Hermitage – and many do. Ranking up there with such museums as the Louvre, the British Museum and the Prado, the Hermitage is arguably the world's finest collection of art. But it wasn't always a museum.

The Hermitage was originally the Winter Palace of the Russian royal family, and was commissioned by the Empress Elizabeth in 1754. Using her beloved Bartolomeo Rastrelli (1700–71) to design the building, she worked with the architect to create a masterpiece of baroque interiors and rococo exteriors.

Catherine the Great hated the baroque touches and remodelled everything to suit her more classical tastes. She bought the first of the museum's collections in 1764; further purchases followed over the next 150 years. The palace was opened as a state museum following Tsar Nicholas II's abdication and the October Revolution in 1917. The Communists saw the palace as a symbol of their years of repression and wanted to create a showcase that the population could be proud of.

Today, the Hermitage collection draws from almost every era of Western art – from the ancient civilisations to the years of post-Impressionism. Its Impressionist rooms are particularly acclaimed, along with its collection of exquisite Fabergé eggs.

Getting into the Hermitage can be a challenge due to the constant queues, so get there as early as possible. The

main entrance is through the courtyard of the palace from Palace Square. Here you will find the ticket and information counters. Admission is steep at R350, but when you see just how big the place is, you'll understand why the cost is so high. All ISIC card holders and children under 17 get in free of charge. If you're tight on time, consider joining one of the English highlight tours that takes visitors through the most impressive rooms in an hour and a half. Trying to do it in a day is a challenge that many attempt and fail. After all, there are more than 1,000 rooms and 110 staircases in this palace composed of five interlocked buildings. Most visitors who want a whistle-stop tour concentrate their efforts on the following rooms:

178–197 The staterooms of the Romanov family
207–215 Florentine Art
217–222 Venetian Art
229 Raphael
244–247 Flemish Art
249–254 Dutch Art
228–238 Italian Art
333–350 Impressionists and post-Impressionists.

To point out all the treasures of the museum could take an entire guidebook. Your best bet is to get a map at the information counter or download one from the website.

The Hermitage ⓐ Dvortsovaya Ploshchad, 2 ⓣ 311 3465 ⓦ www.hermitagemuseum.org ⓛ 10.30–18.00 Tues–Sun; admission charge ⓜ Metro: Gostiny Dvor

🔺 *The Winter Palace now houses the Hermitage art collection*

Vasilevskiy Island

Given as a gift to Prince Menshikov by Peter the Great, Vasilevskiy Island feels very different to the other communities described in this guidebook. Menshikov built his palace on the eastern tip of the island, closest to the city centre – and the buildings that pepper this region feel very much like an extension of Nevsky Prospekt, complete with grandiose constructions and elegant pastel exteriors. As you move further west, however, the architecture changes and large clumps of Soviet-built mass housing complexes come into view.

Many visitors avoid this pocket of the city, and for that they should be rapped on their knuckles! In its early days, the island housed the city's port and commercial centre, and it continues to hold the bulk of the buildings that make up St Petersburg University. Peter the Great originally intended for the island to be his capital, however, the River Neva created too many obstacles to make it viable. During storms, the river would build up, making crossings treacherous, and winter months brought ice that effectively cut off residents from the mainland for large periods of time.

Historians point to Vasilevskiy Island as the cradle of the revolutions of 1905 and 1917. During the years of the Industrial Revolution, many factories were built in this district in close proximity to the university. The combination of a large working class and the growth of fiery student activism created a hotbed for the development of Communist views; the area became known for its militancy.

As the island is so large, sights can be far apart from each other and hard to reach. Only one metro station serves the island, so walks from the station can be long. Prepare to spend a full day exploring if you want to see all the attractions and museums and be sure to wear comfortable shoes. Also, popular museums such as the Museum of Anthropology & Ethnography and the Doll Museum sometimes exhibit collections that aren't suitable for children, so check in advance to ensure that displays are kid-friendly.

SIGHTS & ATTRACTIONS

Menshikov Palace

Menshikov Palace, one of the city's earliest stone structures, was built to house Prince Alexander Menshikov (1673–1729), friend of Peter the Great and the first governor of the city. It is now part of the Hermitage. Though more luxurious than the tsar's palace, it was used by Peter only for official functions, as he preferred the intimacy of the Summer Palace. Avoid the ground floor and head straight upstairs to the first floor for the collection of elegant interiors and original fittings.

ⓐ Universitetskaya Naberezhnaya 15 🕐 10.30–17.00 Tues–Sun; admission charge Ⓜ Metro: Vasileostrovskaya

Pushkin House

Currently home to the Institute of Russian Literature, this house offers exhibits dedicated to some of the greats of the written word, including Tolstoy, Gogol and Gorky. Tours must be booked in advance as casual drop-ins are not permitted.

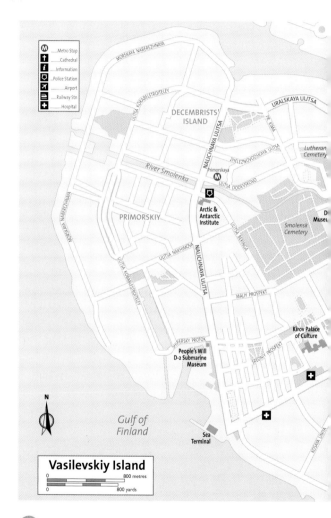

M	Metro Stop
✝	Cathedral
i	Information
◎	Police Station
✈	Airport
🚉	Railway Stn
✚	Hospital

MORSKAYA NABEREZHNAYA

ULITSA KORABELSTROITELEY

URALSKAYA ULITSA

DECEMBRISTS' ISLAND

NALICHNAYA ULITSA

PR. KIMA

Lutheran Cemetery

ZHELEZNOVODSKAYA ULITSA

River Smolenka

Primorskaya **M**

ULITSA ODOEVSKOVO

◎

Arctic & Antarctic Institute

ULITSA BERINGA

PRIMORSKIY

Smolensk Cemetery

D Musei

MOSKAYA NABEREZHNAYA

ULITSA NAKHIMOVA

NALICHNAYA ULITSA

ULITSA KORABLESTROITELEY

MALIY PROSPEKT

Kirov Palace of Culture

SREDNIY PROSPEKT

SHPERSKY PROTOK

People's Will D-2 Submarine Museum

✚

✚

N

Gulf of Finland

Sea Terminal

KOSAYA LINIYA

Vasilevskiy Island

0 ————————— 800 metres
0 ————————— 800 yards

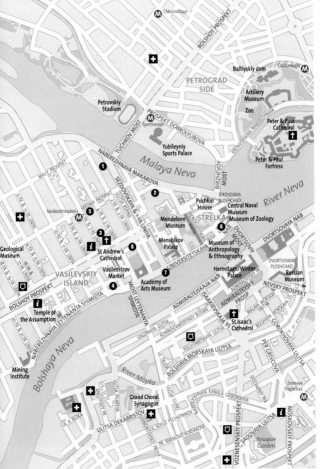

Chkalovskaya

BOLSHOY PROSPEKT

PETROGRAD
SIDE

Baltiyskiy dom

Gorkovskaya

Artillery
Museum

Petrovskiy
Stadium

Zoo

PROSPEKT DOBROLYUBOVA

Sportivnaya

Peter & Paul
Cathedral

Yubileyniy
Sports Palace

Peter & Paul
Fortress

NABEREZHNAYA MAKAROVA

Malaya Neva

River Neva

TUCHKOV MOST

BIRZHEVOY MOST

BIRZHEVAYA
PLOSHCHAD

MALY PROSPEKT

Pushkin
House

Central Naval
Museum

SEZDOVSKAJA & 1-YA LINIYA

Vasileostrovskaya

Mendeleev
Museum

STRELKA

Museum of Zoology

DVORTSOVAYA NAB

Menshikov
Palace

Museum of
Anthropology
& Ethnography

Geological
Museum

St Andrew's
Cathedral

UNIVERSITETSKAYA

DVORTSOVY MOST

DVORTSOVAYA
PLOSHCHAD

Russian
Museum

Vasileostrov
Market

Academy of
Arts Museum

Hermitage/Winter
Palace

NEVSKY PROSPEKT

VASILEVSKIY
ISLAND

ADMIRALTEJSKAJA NAB

ISAAKIEVSKAYA

ADMIRALTEYSKIY
PROSP

BOLSHOY PROSPEKT

Temple of
the Assumption

NABEREZHNAYA LEYTENANTA SHIMIOTA

MOST LEYTENANTA SHIMIOTA

ADMIRALTEJSKAYA NAB

St Isaac's
Cathedral

GALERNAYA ULITSA

KONNOGVARDEYSKIY BULVAR

BOLSHAYA MORSKAYA ULITSA

BOLSHAYA MOSKOVSKAYA

MALAYA MOSKOVSKAYA

PER GRIVCOVA

GOROKHOVAYA ULITSA

Mining
Institute

River Moyka

POCHTAMTSKAYA ULITSA

Bolshaya Neva

NABEREZHNAYA KANALA GRIBOEDOVA

Sennaya
Ploschad

Sennaya
Plaschad

Grand Choral
Synagogue

ULITSA DEKABRISTOV

UL A BLOKA

ANGLISKIY PR

ULITSA PSIRFIA

PER RIMSKOVO-KORSAKOVA

DEKRATNIKOV

VOZNESENSKIY PROSPEKT

SADOVAYA ULITSA

Yusupov
Garden

MOSKOVSKIY PROSPEKT

◆ A tiled interior at the Menshikov Palace

ⓐ Nab. Makarova 4 ☏ 328 1901 ⓦ www.pushkinhouse.spb.ru
🕐 10.00–16.00 Mon–Fri; admission charge Ⓜ Metro:
Vasilostrovskaya

Temple of the Assumption
Built as a church in 1895, this example of neo-Byzantine
architecture was constructed on the site of an early monastery.
Closed in 1934, it reopened almost a quarter-century later after
being transformed into a year-round skating rink.
ⓐ Nab. Leytenanta Shimidta/15–Ya Liniya ☏ 321 7473 🕐 Hours
vary, open daily Ⓜ Metro: Vasileostrovskaya

CULTURE

Academy of Arts Museum
Founded in 1757, this academy trained boys in art from the age of
five until they graduated at 15. The premise behind its creation was
to create a new artist 'super-race' that would use art to benefit the
state – and it succeeded, until students rebelled against the strict
doctrine in 1863. Inside, visitors will find works produced by former
students throughout its many years as an educational institution.
ⓐ Universitetskaya Naberezhnaya 17 ☏ 213 6496 🕐 11.00–18.00
Wed–Sun; admission charge Ⓜ Metro: Vasileostrovskaya

Central Naval Museum
Naval enthusiasts love this museum, which looks at the
history of the Russian navy from its early years to the present.
The most interesting display is a model of the *botik* (boat)
in which Peter the Great learned to sail. The Rostral Columns,

celebrating naval victories, stand either side of the building.

 Birzhevaya Ploshchad 4 328 2502 www.museum.navy.ru 10.30–17.30 Wed–Sun; admission charge Metro: Vasileostrovskaya

Doll Museum

Traditional nesting dolls are just the tip of the iceberg when it comes to traditional doll-making in Russia. This museum showcases the artistry and craftsmanship of the Russian doll industry. Sundays offer interactive doll-making workshops.

 Kamskaya ul 8 327 7224 11.00–18.00 Tues–Sun; admission charge Metro: Vasileostrovskaya

Geological Museum

This museum is a real find for those with kids in tow. Exhibits worth taking the children to include a wealth of dinosaur bones and a map of the Soviet Union made completely out of semiprecious stones. With over one million items on display, they're bound to find something that catches their eye.

 Sredniy Prospekt 74 312 5399 10.00–17.00 Mon–Fri Metro: Vasileostrovskaya

Mendeleev Museum

Failed chemistry students will curse at the sight of this museum dedicated to the man who created the Periodic Table of elements. Others will enjoy seeing his study preserved as it was when he worked there. Look carefully and you may even be able to spot a few early versions of the cornerstone of science.

🔺 *The Rostral Columns commemorate Russian naval victories*

Mendeleevskaya Liniya 2 328 9744 11.00–16.00 Mon–Fri; admission charge Metro: Vasileostrovskaya

Museum of Anthropology & Ethnography

This museum was the first one ever built in Russia. Founded by Peter the Great, it was commissioned to cater to the tsar's rather grim delights. The old anatomy theatre hosts a collection of malformed babies preserved in formaldehyde. Examples include conjoined twins and babies missing limbs and organs. Only for the strong of stomach.

 Universitetskaya Naberezhnaya 3 328 1412
 www.kunstkamera.ru 11.00–17.00 Fri–Wed; admission charge Metro: Vasileostrovskaya

Museum of Zoology

Over 40,000 stuffed animals are on display at this museum, reported to be the largest collection in the world. Exhibits include a complete woolly mammoth, which was thawed out of the Siberian ice in 1902.

 Universitetskaya Naberezhnaya 1/3 218 0112 11.00–18.00 Sat–Thur; admission charge Metro: Vasileostrovskaya

People's Will D-2 Submarine Museum

The D-2 Submarine saw action between the years of 1931 and 1956. During its time, it sank five German warships. To see how the crew of 56 lived inside the tiny structure, you will have to endure a tour that is offered in Russian only.

 Shipersky Protok 10 356 5277 11.00–17.00 Tues–Sun; admission charge Metro: Vasileostrovskaya

RETAIL THERAPY

Shopping streets & markets

Vasilevskiy Island has few shopping opportunities, so it's best to keep your credit cards tucked away while here and take advantage of the better opportunities in the city centre instead. A couple of the better locations in the area to spend a ruble or two are listed below:

Doll Museum The gift shop in the museum of the same name sells dolls created by local designers. It's definitely not the kind of thing to give to a toddler, though, as the craftsmanship and therefore the prices are incredibly high. @ Kamskaya Ulitsa 8

○ *The Museum of Anthropology & Ethnography on Vasilevskiy Island*

① 327 7224 **🕓** 11.00–18.00 Tues–Sun; admission charge **Ⓜ** Metro: Vasileostrovskaya

Vasileostrov Market Currently undergoing a much-needed renovation, this large market hall is the shopping centre for the residents of the area. An outdoor flea market occasionally pops up just outside the entrance, although there is no set schedule. **ⓐ** Bolshoy Prospekt 14/16

TAKING A BREAK

Stolle £ ❶ You won't be able to resist diving into one of the pies on offer at this chic café that has proven a hit with the city's young and funky. Both sweet and savoury varieties are on offer, and can be downed with the excellent coffee **ⓐ** Sezdovskaya/1–Ya Liniya 50 **①** 328 7860 **🕓** 08.30–22.00 **Ⓜ** Metro: Vasileostrovskaya

AFTER DARK

Restaurants
Bogemus £ ❷ Vegetarians beware! This Czech bar serves up the best in meat and dumplings for those looking for something warm and extremely filling. Wash it all down with a bottle (or three) of one of the six Czech brews on offer. Beer parties kick off every Friday night and last until the final customer leaves. **ⓐ** Birzhevoy Proezd 1/10 **①** No phone **🕓** 11.00–01.00 **Ⓜ** Metro: Vasileostrovskaya

Laima £ ❸ For a late-night bite, you can't beat this Russian fast food outlet that offers simple, stodgy yet scrumptious pub grub and gallons of beer choices. ⓐ 6-Ya Liniya 15 ☎ 329 0895 ⏰ 24 hrs Ⓝ Metro: Vasileostrovskaya

Russky Kitsch £–££ ❹ For a taste of true Russian kitsch, head directly to this restaurant serving up dishes ordered from a menu that uses copies of Lenin's writing as inspiration. The décor is pure pop complete with waiters dressed to look like Communist youth. ⓐ Universitetskaya Naberezhnaya 25 ☎ 325 1122 ⏰ 12.00–24.00 Ⓝ Metro: Vasileostrovskaya

Café Rotunda ££ ❺ Parisian bistro food is served up at this comfortable restaurant that's a cut above the low-grade joints that surround it. Enjoy a light lunch of soup and a salad or something heartier such as *steak frites*, Russian-style. ⓐ 5-Ya Liniya 42 ☎ No phone ⏰ 11.00–23.00 Ⓝ Metro: Vasileostrovskaya

Restioran ££ ❻ The perfect place for a spot of romance, this is where to bring your partner for a long lunch or a delicious dinner. The atmosphere will make you feel like you've entered an eatery during the height of the Romanov period. Luckily, the prices are low enough for even the peasant class to afford. ⓐ Tamozhenny Pereulok 2 ☎ 327 8979 ⏰ 12.00–24.00 Ⓝ Metro: Nevsky Prospekt

New Island ££–£££ ❼ Sightsee as you sup on this boat-restaurant that boasts a number of high-profile former guests, including the queen of Spain and President Bush. Meals are

high-quality continental, but don't go expecting anything too adventurous. Cruises last for two hours. Universitetskaya Naberezhnaya/1-Ya Liniya Cruises depart: 14.00, 18.00, 20.00 & 22.30 Metro: Vasilostrovskaya

Ustrichny Bar £££   Expensive, yet high-quality *foie gras,* oysters and champagne. Expect to find a typical clientele of high-class call-girls, *mafiosi,* businessmen with massive expense accounts and brassy *nouveaux riches.* Like something out of a *Dallas* episode – but even more decadent. Bolshoy Prospekt 8 323 2279 www.oysters.spb.ru 12.00–01.00 Metro: Vasilostrovskaya

Bars, clubs & discos
Ostrov
This club caters to a select crowd due to its out-of-the-way location. While the revolving dance floors are a bit naff, the mainly Western pop and techno music makes a change from the Russian pop you find in most other locations. Get a cab from the metro, though, as it's a long walk. Nab. Leytenanta Shimidta 37 328 4857 23.00–04.00 Metro: Vasileostrovskaya

Cinemas & theatres
While Vasilevskiy Island is one of the oldest parts of St Petersburg, it doesn't boast a long history of culture and entertainment. Due to this lack of an artistic community, there are very few cultural institutions of note in this pocket of the city.

RUSSIAN MUSEUM

If the Hermitage were not in the same town as the Russian Museum, then this collection would evoke a lot more interest. A superb museum, filled with the treasures of centuries of Russian artistry, the Russian Museum covers everything from early Orthodox icons to modern art – and everything in between. Its magnificence lies in its breadth rather than in any particular standout pieces: you won't spend your time racing to see a *Mona Lisa*. Instead, you can pause and reflect on Russian art as a whole and its influence on Russian culture.

The museum itself is inside the Mikhailovskiy Palace, which was built over the course of six years from 1819 to 1825 for Grand Duke Mikhail. The grand duke was the brother of Tsars Alexander I and Nicholas I and the palace was a gift to him to make up for the fact that he would never be able to be tsar himself.

The original heart of the collection was made up of treasures owned by Tsar Alexander III and opened to the public in 1898. There are now over 400,000 items, of which only a fraction are on display at any one time.

Attached to the museum is the Benois Wing, built as an extension in the early 20th century. It is accessible via a walkway that runs from Room 48 on the first floor of the main building. The layout of the museum is in approximate date order, with a basic tour starting on the second floor. Once you pass through the main entrance and pay for your ticket, take the grand

staircase up to begin your browsing. The first four rooms focus on early church icons, with subsequent rooms fast-forwarding rapidly into the days of Peter the Great and the Empress Elizabeth.

Rooms 12–17 feature the works of the Academy of Art, with many paintings heavily influenced by the Italian fashions of the day. Modern features also begin to crop up in the form of innovative detail and subject choices.

One of the most interesting sections of the museum is from rooms 23 to 25, where the works of the Wanderers are hung. The Wanderers were a group of Academy students who rebelled against the institution's strict dictates. Instead, they decided to wander amongst the people and paint scenes of everyday rural life – almost like a 19th-century Brueghel.

The main building continues through the 19th century, eventually linking with the Benois Wing where the modern era begins. Periods covered in this extension include Cubism, Futurism, the Early Soviet Period and Socialist Realism – must-sees for anyone interested in delving deeply into Communist culture. Unfortunately for visitors, the collection ends abruptly with works produced in the 1940s, but the number of items on display is so vast that you won't feel cheated by this lack of work from the last few decades.

Russian Museum: ⓐ Inzhenernaya Ulitsa 4 ⓣ 311 1465 ⓦ www.rusmuseum.ru ⓔ 10.00–18.00 Wed–Sun, 10.00–17.00 Mon; admission charge ⓝ Metro: Gostiny Dvor

○ *Trace the history of Russian art at the Russian Museum*

South & East of the Fontanka

South of the Fontanka, there are fewer historical buildings, yet the city buzz remains strong. Here is where the bulk of expansion occurred during the years of Soviet rule, and sights have a distinct leaning towards celebration of this relatively recent era.

SIGHTS & ATTRACTIONS

Alexander Nevsky Monastery & Tikhvin Cemetery

Grave-hunters will love visiting this monastery, final resting place of some of the nation's finest artists. Built in 1713 by Peter the Great, the monastery was mistakenly thought to have been placed on the spot where Alexander of Novgorod beat the Swedes in 1240. The building is open to the public, but it is really the graves that are of most interest. Tombs you can spot include those of Tchaikovsky, Borodin, Mussorgsky and Rimsky-Korsakov.
ⓐ Lavra Alexandra Nevskogo, Ploshchad Alexandra Nevskogo ⓘ 274 0409 ⓛ Monastery: 11.00–18.00 Fri–Wed, Mar–Sept; 11.00–15.30 Fri–Wed, Oct–Feb. Cemetery: 09.30–20.00 Apr–Oct, 09.30–16.00 Nov–Mar; admission charge ⓝ Metro: Ploshchad Alexandra Nevskogo

Beloselsky-Belozersky Palace

While the bulk of this building is closed to the public, a wax museum devoted to historical figures is well worth a visit.
ⓐ Nevsky Prospekt 41 ⓘ 315 5636 ⓛ 11.00–18.30; admission charge ⓝ Metro: Gostiny Dvor

Bolshoy Dom

Locals still walk a little faster when going by this building – it is the former headquarters of the KGB. While it's not possible to go inside, it is still an important site for those looking to examine the years of Communist rule.

ⓐ Liteyniy Prospekt 4 ⓒ Not open to the public ⓝ Metro: Chernyshevskaya

Church of St John of Kronstadt

While this church isn't very important, its Byzantine façade is one of the most impressive in the city. There isn't much to see inside, but it makes for a nice stop.

ⓐ Ulitsa Nekrasova 31 ⓣ 273 9619 ⓒ 09.00–18.00 ⓝ Metro: Mayakovskaya

Guvd Museum

A museum for budding Sherlock Holmeses. This intriguing collection details the history of criminality and law enforcement in the city. Of particular interest is the display looking at the history of mafia involvement in the area. Entrance is by pre-arranged guided tour only.

Ulitsa Poltavskaya 12 ⓣ 279 4233 ⓒ 10.00–17.00 Mon–Fri; admission charge ⓝ Metro: Ploshchad Vosstaniya

Preobrazhenskiy Church (Cathedral of the Transfigurations)

Built by the Empress Elizabeth to honour the Preobrazhenskiy Guards for their support in her bid for power in 1741, this church is now best known as the home of the Kapella Choir, one of the finest in St Petersburg. Performances can be heard during daily

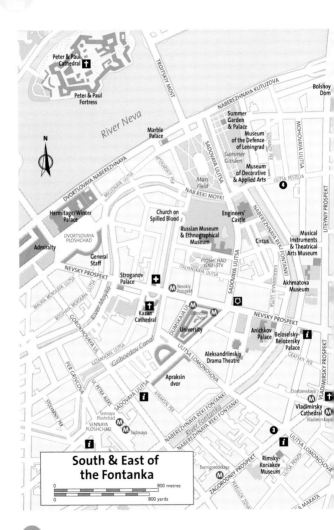

Peter & Paul
Cathedral

Peter & Paul
Fortress

TROITSKIY MOST

NABEREZHNAYA KUTUZOVA

Bolshoy
Dom

River Neva

Marble
Palace

Summer
Garden
& Palace

Museum
of the Defence
of Leningrad

MOHOVAYA ULITSA

N

DVORTSOVAYA NABEREZHNAYA

MILIONNAYA ULITSA

APTEKARSKIY PER.

SADOVAYA ULITSA

Mars
Field

Summer
Garden

Museum
of Decorative
& Applied Arts

ULITSA PESTELYA

NAB REKI MOYKI

LITEYNIY PROSPEKT

Hermitage/Winter
Palace

Church on
Spilled Blood

Engineers'
Castle

Russian Museum
& Ethnographical
Museum

Circus

Musical
Instruments
& Theatrical
Arts Museum

DVORTSOVAYA
PLOSHCHAD

Admiralty

General
Staff

Stroganov
Palace

NEVSKIY PROSPEKT

PLOSHCHAD
ISKUSSTV

ITALYANSKAYA ULITSA

SADOVAYA ULITSA

NABEREZHNAYA REKI FONTANKI

KARAVANNAYA ULITSA

Akhmatova
Museum

MALAYA MORSKAIA ULITSA

BOLSHAYA MORSKAYA ULITSA

River Moyka

Nevskiy
Prospekt

Kazan
Cathedral

University

Gostiny
Dvor

NEVSKIY PROSPEKT

GOROKHOVAYA UL.

KAZANSKAYA ULITSA

DUMSKAIA UL.

Anichkov
Palace

Beloselsky-
Belozersky
Palace

VLADIMIRSKIY PROSPEKT

PER. GRIVCOVA

UL. PETRA ALEKS

Griboedov Canal

Aleksandrinskiy
Drama Theatre

GRAFSKIY PER.

Apraksin
dvor

APRAKSIN PER.

Dostoevskaya

SADOVAYA ULITSA

NABEREZHNAYA REKI FONTANKI

Vladimirsky
Cathedral

Vladimirskaya

SIOVANSKI PER

Sennaya
Ploshchad

SENNAYA
PLOSHCHAD

Sadovaya

River Fontanka

NABEREZHNAYA REKI FONTANKI

ULITSA LOMONOSOVA

Evenigorodskaya

Rimsky-
Korsakov
Museum

ZAGORODNIY PROSPEKT

PEREULOK DZHA

UL. MARATA

South & East of
the Fontanka

0 _____ 800 metres
0 _____ 800 yards

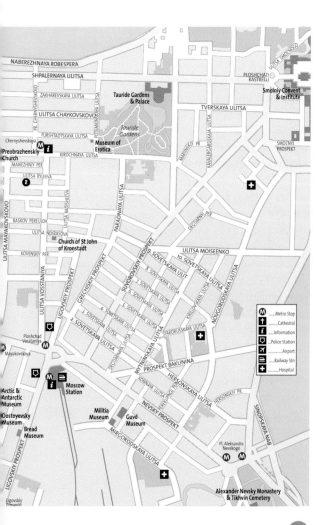

services. Preobrazhenskaya Ploshchad No phone Services: 10.00 & 18.00 Metro: Chernyshevskaya

Smolniy Convent & Institute

Rastrelli created this unparalleled baroque masterpiece that acts as the focal point for a convent. Inside is an art gallery, but the climb to the belfry is the main draw.

 Ploshchad Rastrelli 3/1 271 9182 11.00–17.15 Fri–Wed; admission charge Metro: Chernyshevskaya

Tauride Gardens & Palace

Built as a thank-you gift to Potemkin by Catherine the Great following his successful campaign to capture the Ukraine, the Tauride Palace is now a shell of what it once was, following its transformation into a barracks by Tsar Paul I. Now off-limits to visitors, it sits across a lake from the City Children's Park – a popular place for locals to bring their kids – which has a collection of rather run-down rides to keep children amused.

 Tauride Gardens (City Children's Park) No phone Open daily Metro: Chernyshevskaya

Vladimirsky Cathedral

One of the few working churches that has been restored, this popular place of worship is a fine example of Russian baroque.

 Vladimirsky Prospekt 20 312 1938 08.00–18.00 Metro: Vladimirskaya

CULTURE

Akhmatova Museum

Anna Akhmatova was a leading Russian writer of the early 20th century. This museum includes mementoes of her life, including photos and letters written to other literary luminaries such as Boris Pasternak. A nice slice of typical 20th-century Russian life.

ⓐ Liteyny Prospekt 53 ⓣ 272 2211 ⓛ 10.00–17.30 Tues–Sun; admission charge ⓜ Metro: Mayakovskaya

Arctic & Antarctic Museum

The 1930s were the glory years of polar exploration and this museum takes a look at the period when expeditions into freezing wastelands brought fame and glory to successful explorers. Displays include examples of recovered mammoth skulls and recreations of typical tents and huts used by expedition teams during the period.

ⓐ Marata 24a ⓣ 113 1998. 10.00–18.00 Wed–Sun, closed last Fri of month; admission charge ⓜ Metro: Vladimirskaya

Bread Museum

The availability of bread (or lack thereof) has been one of the key indicators of the state of the economy ever since Peter the Great introduced German bakers to the city and brought in a bread tax. Specially baked loaves are used to celebrate important occasions in the life of every citizen, a tradition that was difficult to maintain during the lean years of Communism.

ⓐ 73 Ligovskiy Prospekt, 4th Floor ⓣ No phone ⓛ 10.00–17.00 Tues–Sat; admission charge ⓜ Metro: Vladimirskaya

Dostoyevsky Museum

Dostoevsky lived in 20 locations around St Petersburg during his lifetime, but it is this flat that has been restored to celebrate his life and achievements. The writer moved here in 1878. He wrote *The Brothers Karamazov* in the study.

ⓐ Kuznechniy Pereulok 5 ⓣ 311 4031 ⓦ www.md.spb.ru
ⓛ 11.00–18.00 Tues–Sun, closed last Wed of month; admission charge ⓝ Metro: Vladimirskaya

Militia Museum

Few visitors are familiar with this museum chronicling the history of the militia from its formation in 1917 to the 1970s. Periods examined include the days when gangsters ruled the streets during the 1920s and the war years when the militia were responsible for the defence of the city. Tours need to be booked in advance.

ⓐ Poltavskaya Ulitsa 12 ⓣ 279 4233 ⓛ 10.00–18.00 Mon–Fri by appointment only; admission charge ⓝ Metro: Ploshchad Vosstaniya

Museum of Decorative & Applied Arts

Stunning examples of tapestries, paintings, furniture, glassware and porcelain, this is now considered one of the finest private collections in Europe. The building, which took ten years to build from 1885 to 1895, is also considered a masterpiece. It is designed in a variety of styles – each room is unique. After the Revolution, many of these rooms fell into disrepair; however, an extensive renovation project is underway, despite a complete lack of funding from government ministries.

ⓐ Solyanoy Pereulok 13 ⓣ 273 3258 ⓛ 11.00–17.00 Tues–Sat; admission charge ⓝ Metro: Chernyshevskaya

Museum of the Defence of Leningrad
When this museum opened three months after the end of the blockade of the city during World War II, it boasted an impressive collection of 37,000 exhibits that kept the memory of the period alive in the minds of the shell-shocked citizens. Three years later,

🔺 *The Sheremetev Palace is home to the Akhmatova Museum*

Stalin closed it down. It wasn't until 1989 that the museum was reopened to the public with a drastically reduced collection. Displays include propaganda posters and an example of the sawdust-filled hunks of bread that locals were forced to exist on.
ⓐ Solyanoy Pereulok 9 ❶ 275 7208 ⓛ 10.00–17.00 Thur–Tues, closed last Thur of month; admission charge Ⓜ Metro: Chernyshevskaya

Museum of Erotica

Housed in a former venereal disease clinic, this museum has a small collection of sexually-themed items, including what is alleged to be Rasputin's preserved penis.
ⓐ Furshtadtskaya Ulitsa 47 ❶ 320 7600 ⓛ 08.00–22.00
Ⓜ Metro: Chernyshevskaya

Musical Instruments & Theatrical Arts Museum

Housed in the Sheremetyev Palace, this museum holds a collection of 19th- and 20th-century instruments, some of which are beautifully decorated. The Sheremetyev family were well-known artistic patrons in the 18th century.
ⓐ Nab. Reki Fontanki 34 ❶ 272 4441 ⓛ 12.00–18.00 Wed–Sun; admission charge Ⓜ Metro: Gostiny Dvor

Rimsky-Korsakov Museum

This museum recreates the look of the home of the composer Rimsky-Korsakov as it appeared during the later years of his life. Back in his day, guests such as Stravinsky and Rachmaninoff came to the flat to perform at Rimsky-Korsakov's weekly salon, held every Wednesday.

🅐 Zagorodniy Prospekt 28 ☏ 113 3208 🕐 11.00–18.00 Wed–Sun; admission charge Ⓝ Metro: Dostoevskaya

RETAIL THERAPY

Anglia Books If you're desperate for a read, this bookshop is the only one in town specialising in English-language selections. Options are limited to contemporary fiction, travel literature and photography – but it is a must-stop for the expat community.
🅐 Nab. Reki Fontanki 38 ☏ 279 9294 🕐 10.00–19.00 Ⓝ Metro: Gostiny Dvor

Kuznechniy Market St Petersburg's most atmospheric market. Stocked full of fruit, veg and local delicacies – it's a treat for the eyes, nose and tastebuds. Pick up delicious honey or sour cream if you want to stock your larder with Russian favourites.
🅐 Kuznechniy Pereulok 3 ☏ 312 4161 🕐 08.00–20.00 Ⓝ Metro: Vladimirskaya

🔺 *Russian dolls come in many guises, from world leaders to Beatles*

Voytenborg

Army surplus store stocking great military-themed souvenirs. Most of the items available are authentic examples of Russian military wear. The quality and price can't be beaten. ⓐ Nevsky Prospekt 67 ❶ 314 6254 ❷ 10.00–18.00 Mon–Fri ⓝ Metro: Mayakovskaya

TAKING A BREAK

Café Vienna ££ ❶ The best cakes in town in an opulent setting. Go if only to see the interiors of this majestic hotel. Expensive for what you get, but worth the splurge. ⓐ Nevsky Palace Hotel, Nevsky Prospekt 57 ❶ 380 2001 ❷ 10.00–24.00 ⓝ Metro: Mayakovskaya

AFTER DARK

Restaurants

Aziya £ ❷ Nicely spiced Uzbek and Russian cuisine. Prices are considered good by local standards so be sure to book in advance. ⓐ Ulitsa Ryleeva 23 ❶ 272 0168 ❷ 11.00–23.00 ⓝ Metro: Cheryshevskaya

Shinok £–££ ❸ Campy Ukrainian fast food dished up by waiters in Ukrainian peasant gear. ⓐ Zagorodniy Prospekt 13 ❶ 571 8262 ❷ 24 hrs ⓝ Metro: Dostoevskaya

Chornaya Koska, Bely Kot ££–£££ ❹ Ultra-chic eatery with exposed brick walls and films shown on a giant screen to add to

the art-house atmosphere. The house specialty is roast suckling pig, but you don't have to (and probably can't afford to) order it. ⓐ Ulitsa Pestelya 13/15 ❶ 279 7430 🕒 12.00–24.00 Ⓜ Metro: Chernyshevskaya

Bars, clubs & discos
Jet Set International DJs are often brought into this elite club with a strict guest-list policy. Dress to impress and come loaded with a fat wallet. ⓐ Furshtatskaya Ulitsa 58B 🕒 23.00–06.00 Ⓜ Metro: Chernyshevskaya

Red Club Enjoy the alternative music scene at this club located in a converted warehouse ⓐ Poltavskaya Ulitsa 7 ❶ 277 1366 🕒 22.30–late Ⓜ Metro: Ploshchad Vosstaniya

Sunduk Intimate Jazz and Blues club with a casual feel. ⓐ Furshtatskaya Ulitsa 42 ❶ 272 3100 🕒 12.00–23.00 Ⓜ Metro: Chernyshevskaya

Cinemas & theatres
Bolshoy Drama Theatre This theatre was one of the first to be built in the city and remains one of its grandest. Expect high-quality performances that tend towards the conservative. ⓐ Nab Reki Fontanki 65 ❶ 310 9242 Ⓜ Metro: Sennaya Ploshchad

Bolshoy Puppet Theatre The city's main puppet theatre has 16 shows geared for children in its repertoire; it is a great place to bring youngsters when they get museumed-out. ⓐ Ulitsa Nekrasova 10 ❶ 272 8215 Ⓜ Metro: Chernyshevskaya

THE PETER & PAUL FORTRESS

You would think that a fortress as impressive as this one could boast of a history filled with the scars of battle and wartime success – but you'd be wrong. At the time of its building, the greatest foe the nation had were the Swedes, but skirmishes with the Scandinavian enemy ended just before the fortress was completed in 1703, immediately banishing the building's use as a defensive structure to obsolescence.

Peter the Great built this structure, the oldest in the city, with the intention of developing his fledgling city around it. Had his dreams been realised, the city centre would look very different from how it does today, situated primarily on the opposite bank of the river from its present position. Challenges faced during the construction of the fortress convinced city planners that a new location was required, and St Petersburg was shifted to compensate.

The fortress is well positioned to defend the city against marauding forces, due to the fact that the banks of the Neva rise immediately in front of the building, making any passing ships easy prey for the powerful cannons. Unfortunately, military tacticians believe its star shape would not have provided much security.

In order to find a use for it, subsequent tsars transformed the palace into a military and political prison, a job it continued to perform until 1917. Peter the Great's own son, Alexei, was the prison's first resident. Rumours abound that his screams can still be heard after dark.

Revolutionaries hated the building, associating its solid features with the repressive regal regime. Many anti-tsarist forces referred to the place as 'Russia's Bastille', using French Revolutionary terminology to spur the peasant classes into overthrowing the tsar and his family. This plan eventually worked, as stories of the various torture techniques leaked from the fortress, repulsing even the most hardened of citizens. Following the 1917 uprising, the Peter & Paul Fortress was never used to incarcerate people again.

🔺 *Fortress and fountains: the Peter & Paul*

Tsarist links remain in the baroque cathedral in the grounds of the fortress: the church is the final resting place of many of the Romanov royal family members, including the family of Nicholas II and Peter the Great himself. This draws many monarchists to the grounds, who burn candles and pray for the return of the royal family.

Also of interest is the Nevsky Gate to the south, which once served as the gateway for prisoners as they were loaded onto boats for execution. Step outside the gate for wonderful views of the riverfront, or join city sunbathers as they catch some rays during the summer months: it's a popular inner-city beach, though submersing oneself in the polluted waters of the Neva is not generally to be recommended.

Peter & Paul Fortress: ☎ 238 4540 🕐 10.00–18.00 Thurs–Mon, 10.00–16.00 Tues; entrance to grounds free, admission charge for museums only Ⓜ Metro: Gorkovskaya

▶ *The grand cascade at Peterhof*

Imperial palaces

You would think that sights as glorious as the imperial palaces that surround the city of St Petersburg would have been exploited as a major tourist Mecca. It's true each palace gets its fair share of visitors, but if you're looking to spend more than a day at any of these splendid examples of regal splendour, you'd be advised to think again. In most cases, there are no hotels – or even cafés – serving the needs of tourists. Dining options are often limited to the overpriced facilities found on the palace grounds, and even in those cases opening hours can be limited – so bring food with you if you want to be sure of sustenance.

If the palaces are near the top of your 'must-see' list, then arrange your visit between late spring and early autumn. Palace gardens are just as inspiring as the palaces themselves (especially in the case of Peterhof) and you'll want to see them in decent weather.

GATCHINA

Originally home to the sister of Peter the Great, this palace – located 45 km (28 miles) southwest of the city – eventually fell into the hands of Grigory Orlov as a thank-you gift from his lover, Catherine the Great, for his role in the assassination of her husband, Peter III. While the palace remains impressive, it is one of the least inspiring of St Petersburg's collection of noble retreats, as few of the rooms are restored.

Instead, head for the lake, with its meandering trails, soothing bridges, forests of birch trees and secluded islands. The romantic interludes that must have taken place in these

manicured surroundings would surely shock contemporary visitors – especially in the Birch House, which features a frontage constructed from halved birch logs.

Gatchina was the location of the final home to the Provisional Government, whose leader Kerensky fled here in the early hours of 25 October 1917 in order to avoid the slaughter at the Winter Palace. Later, he escaped the palace confines by disguising himself as a sailor.

During World War II, the Nazis savaged the place. Luckily, most of the treasures had been saved by dedicated staff before the Germans arrived. Watercolours painted in the 1870s are helping restorers bring back a bit of the palace's former glory. ⓐ Gatchina Palace ⓣ 271 13492 ⓛ 10.00–18.00 Tues–Sun; admission charge

GETTING THERE

Take the 431 bus from Moskovskaya station to Gatchina town. The journey lasts about an hour and will cost R25. Alternatively take any train in the direction of Oranienbaum from Baltiisky Station and disembark at Gatchina.

TAKING A BREAK

Dom Khleba £ This bakery and café serves simple snacks that are a lot more edible than those at nearby locations. ⓐ Ulitsa Gobornaya 2 ⓣ No phone ⓛ Hours vary according to season

Shankai Kafe £ They call it Chinese food, but it's not like any you've ever ordered. Better than most other eateries in town

– just don't go in with any expectations. ❷ Ulitsa Gobornaya 15 ❶ No phone ❹ Hours vary according to season

ORANIENBAUM

Peter the Great's best friend, Prince Menshikov, built this palace, and it is a testament to his narcissism. He began construction of it at approximately the same time that Peter began building Peterhof. Menshikov intended the palace to dwarf its nearby competitor.

The name Oranienbaum was given to the palace following the planting of a number of orange trees in the Lower Park. The trees needed constant care and attention in the freezing climate, and were emblematic of Menshikov's love of flaunting his wealth. Unfortunately, Menshikov reached too far and the project bankrupted him; the palace fell into the hands of the Crown. It eventually became the home of Tsar Peter III, husband to Catherine the Great.

Compared to Peterhof and Tsarkoe Selo, the palace of Oranienbaum is badly in need of restoration. Its gardens, however, are filled with delightful pockets of wonder, especially in the Lower Park.

A second palace was built on the grounds by Peter III – a folly constructed to satisfy the tsar's passion for all things military. The interiors at this palace are much more impressive. Then there is the whimsy of the Chinese Palace, constructed by Catherine the Great. Probably the most interesting of the palaces on the grounds at Oranienbaum, this rococo masterpiece features the finest parquet floors, Venetian paintings and marble. It is only when you reach the Buglework

○ *Oranienbaum was named after the orange trees in its grounds*

Room that you spot the minor influences that gave the structure an Oriental flavour. The Small and Large Chinese Rooms of the West Wing showcase the theme in greater detail.
ⓐ Oranienbaum ⓣ 423 1627 ⓒ 10.00–17.00 Wed–Mon, May–Oct; admission charge

GETTING THERE

Take a minibus from outside Artovo metro station or one of the trains running from Baltic station to Oranienbaum-I.

⬥ Pavlovsk Great Palace has been extensively restored

The journey time is anything from 45 minutes to an hour. Bring food with you and don't plan on staying, as there are no eating or sleeping facilities in the surrounding area.

PAVLOVSK

In this city of palaces, Pavlovsk is successful simply due to its location. A trip to the grounds has been a popular day-excursion ever since the 19th century when the completion of a railway line linked it with the city and opened up the region to the bourgeois of St Petersburg.

Compared with other locations, Pavlovsk simply doesn't stack up, especially after World War II saw much of its architecture destroyed. Restoration is ongoing. In fact, it took the Russian government over a quarter of a century just to get the building back into a state where visitors could tour the building. When the Soviets first returned to the area, the roof had caved in, leaving the interiors exposed to the ravages of weather and war.

If you do decide to visit, make sure to mark it down as one of your first palace stops. If viewed after the much grander attractions at Tsarkoe Selo or Peterhof, it could seem a bit of a disappointment – but this is not to say it isn't worth seeing.

One reason it looks and feels so much simpler may be its lack of association with Catherine the Great or Peter the Great. These two rulers had a reputation for intrigue, flamboyance, extravagance and major Machiavellian tendencies – and their homes reflected their personalities. Pavlovsk was owned by Catherine's son, the eventual Tsar Paul, who lived here with his second wife Maria. A glance inside the State Rooms will

give you a peek at the embroidery for which Tsarina Maria was famous for. ☎ 470 2155 Ⓦ www.pavlovskart.spb.ru 🕐 10.00–17.00 Sat–Thur, closed first Fri of every month

GETTING THERE

From St Petersburg, take minibus K-186 from Moskovskaya Ploshchad directly to the palace (which takes an hour), or take the suburban train from Vitebsk station. This takes 35 minutes, but there is a 20-minute walk to the palace from Pavlovsk station. Once again, eating or sleeping in the area is not advised, so plan on bringing a picnic lunch and returning home at the end of your visit.

PETERHOF

This is it – the big one! If you have time to visit only one palace near St Petersburg, then this is the one to head for. Founded by Peter the Great, Peterhof was the first imperial palace to be built outside St Petersburg.

Peter wanted a palace that he could access by sea; one that could rival Versailles, with fantastic gardens. The plans were so grandiose that the final touches weren't completed until the reign of Catherine the Great, who adored the white and gold exterior of the building. Inside, the palace is lavishly decorated, with tons of gilt, ceiling frescoes, and suites dripping in Chinese silk, porcelain and furnishings.

The gardens are the highlight of any visit, littered with fountains and water features that dazzle and delight. The focal point is the Neptune Fountain, an ornate gusher built in the 1650s to celebrate the end of the Thirty Years' War and later

◆ *Peterhof is the most magnificent of the imperial palaces*

brought here. The Grand Cascade and Sea Channel, flanked by fountains, are also spectacular. Children particularly love the Lower Park, where a series of joke fountains shoot water into the unsuspecting faces of their parents.

Be sure to take a detour into Monplaisir, an additional palace in the Peterhof grounds, which was designed by Peter the Great himself. The building is supposed to evoke Holland; Peter lived there in 1697 in order to learn the art of shipbuilding and became very fond of it.

ⓐ Peterhof ⓣ 427 9527 ⓛ 11.00–18.00 Tues–Sun (Monplaisir closed Oct–Apr); admission charge

GETTING THERE

The most picturesque way to get to Peterhof is by hydrofoil from the jetty at St Petersburg's Hermitage. Alternatively, take bus 424 or 103 from Leninsky Prospekt metro. The trip takes no longer than 30 minutes.

TAKING A BREAK

Café Gallereya £–££ Eatery on the ground floor of the Grand Palace, facing the Grand Cascade. Food isn't all that stunning, and tour groups often pack the place out. ⓐ Grand Palace ⓣ 427 7068 ⓛ 10.00–20.00

Morskoy Restaurant ££ Seafood specialities served up in a restaurant with a rustic nautical theme. Near the Museum of Collections. ⓣ 427 5225 ⓛ 12.00–24.00

STRELNA

Strelna could have been wonderful if only Mother Nature played along with the ambitions of Peter the Great. This is the site that Peter originally selected for his imperial palace. Unfortunately, after five years of building work, he discovered that he couldn't create the powerful fountains he wanted unless he installed a series of pumps, so construction began anew at Peterhof.

There are two palaces here: the Wooden Palace and the Konstantin Palace. Following World War II, both were almost completely ruined, and remained in a state of disrepair until a decision was made during the 1990s to restore the Wooden Palace. The Konstantin Palace had to wait until President Putin came to power; then money poured in to rebuild it. In 2003 the newly restored baroque palace played host to the 50 heads of state who came to celebrate the 300th birthday of St Petersburg; it was also the setting for the G8 summit in 2006.

Of the two buildings, the Wooden Palace is definitely the more interesting for visitors. Intimate compared to the constructions at Peterhof and Oranienbaum, the Wooden Palace feels incredibly liveable in as a result of its diminutive size. In contrast, the Konstantin Palace is not easy for visitors to see. Often closed for state events, or for presidential visits, it is off-limits for large portions of the year. If you want to visit, be sure to fax the names of all potential visitors, their passport numbers and country of issue, desired language, date of tour and a contact telephone number to ☏ 438 5884 at least six weeks in advance.

Konstantin Palace, Strelna: ☎ 438 5351. Admission by application only. Closed Wed

Wooden Palace, Strelna: ☎ 438 5351 ⏱ 10.30–17.00. Closed Mon and last Tues of each month; admission charge

GETTING THERE

From St Petersburg, take the train to Strelna station, or minibus K-224, K-300, K-420 or K-424 from Artovo metro station.

TSARSKOE SELO

Second only to Peterhof in terms of importance, Tsarkoe Selo was the final home of the doomed Romanov clan. The palace was loved by Catherine the Great, who spent most of her summers in its confines after inheriting it in 1762. Due to the opulence of the palace, restoration has been ongoing since it was looted by the Germans during World War II. Almost every room was rendered uninhabitable during this period, forcing the Soviets to spend millions in order to restore it to its former state.

The sheer expense and scale of such an undertaking means that the 50+-year restoration is still in full swing. Large sections of the south wing remain closed to the public, including the private apartments of Catherine the Great. The areas that are open offer much to delight, particularly the magnificent Amber Room in the northern wing, which features walls sheeted almost entirely in amber surrounding a mosaic representing the Five Senses made from onyx, lapis lazuli, quartz, jasper and agate. This room was one of the most difficult in the palace to reconstruct, taking 21 years to complete.

If you have the time, step outside to explore the 566-hectare (1,400-acre) Catherine Park and compare the styles of the English, French and Italian gardens.

② Tsarskoe Selo **☎** 466 6699 **🕐** 10.00–16.30 Wed–Mon, closed last Mon of the month

▲ *The stunning blue exterior of the Catherine Palace, Tsarskoe Selo*

GETTING THERE

Take the suburban train from Vitebsk station or minibus K-286, K-287, K-299 or K-342 from Moskovskaya Ploshchad. Journey time is 30–45 minutes.

TAKING A BREAK

Café Kolobok £ Cheap soup, salads and *bliny*. Good for a bite on the go. ⓐ Oranzhernaya 29 ⓘ No phone ⓛ 09.00–21.00

Staraya Bashnya ££ Popular Russian restaurant with just four tables – so you'll need to book ahead. Quaintly located in an old watchtower. ⓐ Akadenichesky Prospekt 14 ⓘ 466 6698 ⓛ 12.00–22.00

ACCOMMODATION

Catherine Hotel ££ Beat the crowds by checking into this hotel the night before you visit Tsarkoe Selo. Rooms feature en-suite bathrooms and fantastic views of the palace. ⓐ Tsarkoe Selo ⓘ 466 8042

Baltic Star Hotel £££ There aren't any decent places to eat in Strelna, but there is certainly a nice place to rest your head. Opened for the Russia-EU summit in 2003, this is an opulent hotel suitable for the most demanding of guests ⓐ Strelna ⓘ 438 5700 ⓦ www.balticstar-hotel.ru

Novgorod & Vyborg

These historic towns make for interesting excursions. Both are around three hours (though in different directions) from St Petersburg.

NOVGOROD

Novgorod was the regal capital during the medieval period and still boasts some fine architecture. While the view of the tower blocks as you enter the city might be a little off-putting, don't worry, as the centre of Novgorod is filled with sights.

GETTING THERE

To visit independently, either take one of the buses that leave every two hours from the Obvodniy Canal bus station or a train from either Vitebsk or Moscow station. The first bus of the day departs at 07.30 and takes about 3½ hours. The last return journey leaves Novgorod at 18.30. The train leaves Vitebsk at 08.30 and takes five hours. From Moscow station the train leaves at 17.20 and takes just three hours. If driving, take the M-10 motorway south out of St Petersburg towards Moscow. Novgorod is about 186 km (116 miles) from St Petersburg and should take around three hours, depending on traffic.

SIGHTS & ATTRACTIONS

Kremlin

The Kremlin was the original fortress of the Russian court

● *The Kremlin and St Sophia's Cathedral*

during medieval times. Built in the 14th century to replace the wooden ramparts erected by Prince Vladimir three centuries earlier, it is an impressive building that resembles the Moscow Kremlin due to its impressive red-brick walls.

ⓐ Kremlin ⓣ 81622 736 08 ⓛ 06.00–24.00 Mon–Sun

St Sophia's Cathedral

This church is the earliest remaining in Novgorod, and has been the city's chief landmark since the 11th century. During the Soviet era, the church fell into disrepair. Only a few original features now remain, but they give you a flavour of its past.

ⓐ Kremlin ⓣ No phone ⓛ 08.00–13.00, 14.00–20.00

Yaroslav's Court

This collection of medieval buildings stands where the former

palace of Yaroslav the Wise once existed. The most important structure is the Cathedral of St Nicholas. Other buildings worth exploring include the Church of the Holy Women, Church of St Procopius and Church of St Paraskeva.

ⓐ Yaroslav's Court ⓣ No phone ⓐ Hours vary for each church; however, the court is accessible 24 hours

TAKING A BREAK

Cafés

Aziya £ A simple café serving Central Asian and Korean dishes. The outdoor *shashlyk* grill is deservedly popular during the summer. ⓐ Yakoleva Ulitsa 22/1 ⓣ 81622 722 27 ⓛ 12.00–02.00

Restaurants

Privdore £–££ Top-quality Russian food that suffers only due to the poor service. Weekday lunches offer great budget specials. ⓐ Lyudogoshaya Ulitsa 3 ⓣ 81622 743 333 ⓛ 12.00–24.00 Mon–Sat

Detinets ££ Slightly tacky themed medieval restaurant specialising in authentic recipes from the period. ⓐ Pokrovskaya Tower, Kremlin ⓣ 81622 746 24 ⓛ 12.00–17.00, 19.00–23.00

ACCOMMODATION

Intourist £–££ Typically uninviting Soviet-era hotel, heavy on the concrete. Rooms are clean, though, and offer nice

river views. Bathrooms are basic. ⓐ Velikaya Ulitsa 16
ⓘ 81622 742 36

Beresta Palace ££ Considered the finest hotel in town, though
that's not saying much. But it has a swimming pool, tennis
courts, a nightclub and buffet breakfast. ⓐ Studentcheskaya
Ulitsa 2a ⓘ 8162 158 010

VYBORG

This historic town is known for its art nouveau architecture,
developed during its heyday when it was part of Finland. The old
quarter is filled with prime examples of homes typical of Baltic
communities and sparse Lutheran churches. When visiting, keep
an eye on your belongings at all times and stay away from the
settlements outside city limits.

GETTING THERE

The easiest way to reach Vyborg is by *elektrichka* train from
Finland station. It takes about an hour and three-quarters to
reach the city. There are also regular trains that take three hours.
Alternatively, take a bus from the Obvodniy Canal station,
though departure times are often inconvenient, making the
train the wisest option.

Drivers have a few options. The fastest and most convenient
(yet least scenic) route is the M-10 Scandinavia Highway
running northwest out of the city. Prepare yourself for a three-
to four-hour journey.

SIGHTS & ATTRACTIONS

Park Monrepos

This stunning garden was originally designed in 1759 by Commandant Stupishin. Its inspiration lies in its use of the coastline to highlight the beauty of its collection of native trees and dainty pavilions. A lack of funds means that some parts of it are in disrepair, giving the location a 'secret garden' feel to it.
ⓐ Park Monrepos **ⓣ** 81378 205 39; admission charge

Stone City

Buildings to look out for in this old quarter of town include the Transfiguration Cathedral and Saints Peter and Paul Cathedral.

Vyborg Castle

The city's main sight is this castle on an island in the bay located below the historic Stone City. Originally built in the late 13th century, the structure remained an important military feature until 1812, when the city was transferred to the Finnish people.

Recaptured by the Soviets in 1939, it came under Finnish control again during World War II, eventually falling back to the Russians by the time the war ended. Today, it hosts regular mock battles, telling the story of its war-scarred past.
ⓐ Vyborg Castle **ⓣ** 81378/215 15 **ⓛ** 10.00–19.00 Tues–Sun; admission charge

TAKING A BREAK

Slavyanskaya £ Atmospheric cellar-restaurant in the Stone City.

Quietly kitsch, it's a good place to try tasty – and hearty – Russian dishes. ⓐ Trapeza Ulitsa Yuzhniy val 4/2 ❶ 81278/932 99

AFTER DARK

Restaurants

Kruglaya Bashnya £–££ The Russian and Finnish cuisine is good here, but it's the restaurant's location at the top of the Round Tower that draws the crowds. ⓐ Rynochnaya Ploshchad ❶ 81278 306 00 🕒 12.00–01.00

Baltic Park ££–£££ Offers French and Russian cuisine that wouldn't particularly turn heads in St Petersburg but is a cut above most of the other eateries in this city. ⓐ Druzhba Hotel, Zheleznodorozhaya Ulitsa 5 ❶ 81278 257 44 🕒 12.00–01.00

ACCOMMODATION

BAT ££ Serviceable, good-value hotel. Ask for a non-smoking room if you don't like the idea of nicotine-stained walls. Book a week in advance and save up to 70 per cent off the normal rate. ⓐ Ulitsa Nikolaev 3 ❶ 81378 345 37 ⓦ www.bathotel.ru

Druzhba ££ Chain hotel with standard amenities. The restaurant is recommended. ⓐ Zheleznodorozhaya Ulitsa 5 ❶ 81278 257 44

⊙ *Finding your way round the city*

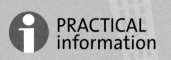

Directory

GETTING THERE
By air

There are two airports that serve St Petersburg. The international airport for travellers from outside the Russian Federation is known as Pulkovo-2 and is located 17 km (10½ miles) south of the city centre. Passengers arriving in St Petersburg from other cities in the Russian Federation will arrive at the domestic airport, Pulkovo-1, approximately 15 km (9 miles) south of the city. The average flying time from London is three and a half hours. See page 48 for more details on airports.

Many people are aware that air travel emits CO_2, which contributes to climate change. You may be interested in the possibility of lessening the environmental impact of your flight through the charity Climate Care, which offsets your CO_2 by funding environmental projects around the world. Visit
ⓦ www.climatecare.org

By rail

Travelling by rail to Russia is a challenge from the UK, but it does allow you to see the bulk of the European continent on the way. The easiest route takes travellers to Brussels on Eurostar followed by a change of train to Berlin. From there, the journey will head to Belarus and up into Russia. Be prepared for two changes of train along the way, and arm yourself with both a Russian visa and a transit visa for Belarus before you depart. The total journey time is approximately 60 hours. The monthly *Thomas Cook European Rail Timetable* has up-to-date schedules

for European international and domestic train services.

Eurostar reservations (UK) ☎ 08705 186 186
ⓦ www.eurostar.com

Thomas Cook European Rail Timetable (UK) ☎ 01733 416 477;
(USA) ☎ 1 800 322 3834 ⓦ www.thomascookpublishing.com

By car

You have to be a pretty determined driver to arrive in St Petersburg by road. Many drivers in Russia purchase a licence rather than passing a test – combine this with the heavy traffic in urban centres and you have a recipe for disaster.

Driving time to St Petersburg from the UK could take at least four to seven days. The most direct route takes you to the city via Sweden and Finland, beginning your journey on the Newcastle–Gothenburg ferry.

To drive on Russian streets you will need to bring your home driving licence, an international driving licence with a Russian-language insert, your passport and visa, a customs document stating that you will take the car back home (unless you are driving a vehicle rented in Russia), an insurance certificate from your home insurer, the vehicle registration certificate, a fire-extinguisher and a first-aid kit. If you are stopped by the police at any time – and you will be – and you don't have any one of these items, you will be subject to a heavy fine.

By bus

It is possible to reach St Petersburg by bus from the UK. From London by Eurolines, the fastest journey time is about 65 hours, depending on connections ⓦ www.eurolines.co.uk

ENTRY FORMALITIES

Visitors to the Russian Federation who are citizens of the UK, Ireland, Australia, the US, Canada, South Africa and New Zealand will need a passport and a visa for stays of up to 30 days (29 days for US citizens). Applications will need to be made through the Russian embassy in your country of residence. Addresses for the Russian Embassy in your country can be found below:

Australia @ 78 Canberra Ave, Griffith, Canberra, ACT 2603 ☎ 02/6295 9474

Canada @ 52 Range Rd, Ottawa, Ontario K1N 8J5 ☎ 613 336 7220

Ireland @ 186 Orwell Rd, Rathgar, Dublin 14 ☎ 01/492 3492

New Zealand @ 57 Messines Road, Karori, Wellington ☎ 04/476 6742

South Africa @ 316 Brooks Street, Menlo Park, Pretoria 0001 ☎ (2712) 362 1337

UK @ 5 Kensington Palace Gardens, London W8 4QS ☎ 020 7229 8027

US @ 2641 Tunlaw Road, NW, Washington, DC 20007 ☎ 202 939 8907

CUSTOMS

Customs regulations are slightly more relaxed these days, but you will still be subject to searches and x-rays on entering and leaving the country. It is a good idea to declare everything you have on you of value, including (but not limited to) laptops, mobile phones and foreign currency. If you use any medicines that require hypodermic needles, you will need to declare them and show your prescription. Export rules are much tougher. If

you purchase any artwork, samovars or jewellery that look even slightly old, you must verify that you can leave the country with the items by consulting the Ministry of Culture ⓐ Malaya Morskaya ul. 17 ① 311 0302. When possible, ask the vendor of the item to complete the paperwork for you. Other items subject to export controls include books published before 1960, which need permission for export from the Russian National Library, and caviar. You are allowed to take out 250g of black caviar and unlimited amounts of red.

MONEY

The currency in Russia is the ruble. Following a crash in 1998, the currency has remained stable; however, most large international hotels and boutiques quote prices in US dollars. A ruble is divided into 100 kopeks – but the kopek is pretty worthless. Currency denominations are: 1,000 rubles, 500 rubles,

● Velo-taxis are a nifty way for visitors to get around

100 rubles, 50 rubles, 10 rubles, 5 rubles, and coins of 5 rubles, 2 rubles, 1 ruble, 50 kopeks, 10 kopeks and 5 kopeks. For years the ruble was a controlled currency. While this is no longer the case, you will still need to fill out a currency declaration form.

Traveller's cheques in US dollars are the best option for travel in Russia. Reliance on ATMs is not advised, as power fluctuations and scams can cause problems for visitors.

The most widely accepted credit cards are Mastercard and Visa. American Express and Diners Club cards are less commonly permitted. Many smaller businesses, including some restaurants, taverns, smaller hotels and most market stalls do not accept credit card payments. This is especially true outside the main cities of St Petersburg and Moscow. Always carry a small amount of cash to cover your day's purchases.

HEALTH, SAFETY & CRIME

Unlike other European locations, you will have to take a few precautions when travelling in Russia. While the water is filtered, it comes from the heavily polluted Neva river, and the filtration system is extremely old. Be safe and stick to bottled water, even when brushing your teeth.

Pharmacies (*apteka*) are marked by a green cross. Russian pharmacists are well stocked with both foreign and domestic products, but language might be an issue if you need advice.

Crime in Russia can be pretty bad, and those from ethnic minorities and wealthy tourists seem particularly targeted. Try and blend with the locals and keep cash, cameras and valuables out of sight at all times. Petty theft (bag-snatching, pick-pocketing) is the most common form of trouble for tourists.

Strolling around the inner city at night can be unsafe. Never walk alone and take taxis if necessary. Your hotel will warn you about particular areas to avoid.

For details of emergency numbers, refer to the 'Emergencies' section on page 137.

OPENING HOURS

Most businesses open Monday–Saturday from 09.00–18.00 or 19.00 with an hour off at some point during the day. Food stores sometimes stay open 24 hours, but you will only find these in residential districts.

Cultural institutions close for one day per week, but not consistently on the same day. Standard hours are 10.00 or 11.00–17.00.

The main post office's opening hours are Mondays–Saturdays from 09.00–19.45 and Sundays from 10.00–17.45.

TOILETS

There are very few public toilets available – and what ones there are, you wouldn't want to use. Use of toilets in restaurants and hotels is generally accepted. Otherwise, branches of international fast-food chains are a good option. It's a good idea to have a stash of toilet paper on hand in case of emergencies.

CHILDREN

While Russians love children, the city of St Petersburg isn't exactly child friendly. Most artistic events are only shown in Russian, local playgrounds aren't well maintained, nappy-changing facilities are non-existent, public breastfeeding is

heavily frowned upon and menus can be off-putting. If you need to find somewhere offering fare more familiar to most Western children, look for branches of the big international fast-food chains or local eateries such as Laima or Patio Pizza.

Nappies and other baby articles are readily obtained from 24-hour shops in residential districts, or from *apteka* (pharmacies).

Try the following child-friendly places:

- **Peterhof** Kids love the joke fountains that spray visitors unexpectedly. Prepare to get wet and giggled at. ⓐ Petrodvorets ⓣ 427 9527 ⓦ www.peterhof.org. Palace: ⓛ 11.00–18.00 Tues–Sun. Fountains and gardens: ⓛ 11.00–19.00 from last weekend in May to September; admission charge

- **Small Academy of Arts** Good for children under 12, it teaches youngsters about themselves and the world beyond. It also has a puppet theatre and playground. ⓐ Nab Reki Fontanki ⓣ 273 2062 ⓛ Hours vary but the centre always closes during the summer months ⓝ Metro: Gostiniy Dvor

- **Wonder Island** The newest fun park in St Petersburg, offering well-maintained dodgems and roller coasters – just don't go expecting Thorpe Park ⓐ Krestovskiy Island ⓣ 323 9707 ⓦ www.divo-ostrov.ru ⓛ 15.00–22.00 Mon, 12.00–22.00 Tues–Fri, 11.00–22.00 Sat–Sun ⓝ Metro: Gorkovskaya

COMMUNICATIONS

Phones

Coin-operated public phones are rare: far more common are card-operated phones. Telephone cards can be bought at any post office and some shops, such as bookshops, or kiosks at railway stations. These cards are really only useful for local calls. Alternatively, purchase a BCL card for international communication. While the quality varies, it is still much better than direct dialling from your hotel room. The cheapest option is a visit to a communications centre, of which there is one in every district.

DIALLING CODES

When making an international call, dial 8 and then wait for the tone to change, follow this with 10 and then the country code, city code (omitting the first 0 if there is one) and then the number. The international dialling code for calls from Russia to Australia is 61, to the UK 44, to the Irish Republic 353, to South Africa 27, to New Zealand 64, and to the USA and Canada 1.

The code to dial Russia from abroad, after the access code, is 7. To call St Petersburg from within Russia dial 812 and then the number.

Post

Postal services can be slow and unreliable. If you are sending a large parcel, avoid branch post offices as they may not have the facilities to service you. Stamps can be bought at the numerous post offices. Postcards sent anywhere in the world cost 10R, and letters cost 14R.

Central Post Office @ Pochtamtskaya ul 9 ❶ 312 7460
🕓 09.00–19.45 Mon–Sat, 10.00–17.45 Sun Ⓜ Metro: Sadovaya

Internet

Internet access is easy to come by around the city. There are numerous internet cafés to choose from, although connections can be temperamental depending on the daily state of the city's telephone system.

Two recommended locations are:

FM Club @ ul Dostoevskogo 6A ❶ 277 1872 🕓 08.00–22.00
Ⓜ Metro: Vladmirskaya

Red Cloud @ Kazanskaya ul 30–32 ❶ 595 4138 🕓 11.00–08.00
Ⓜ Metro: Sennaya Pl

ELECTRICITY

The standard electrical current is 220 volts. Two-pin adaptors can be purchased at most electrical shops.

TRAVELLERS WITH DISABILITIES

Facilities for visitors with disabilities are very poor in Russia, partly due to a historic disregard of the problem and partly to lack of finance. Access ramps are rare. One exception is the Hermitage, which offers good wheelchair access.

Useful websites include:

Ⓦ www.sath.org (US-based site)

Ⓦ www.access-able.com (general advice on worldwide travel)

http://travel.guardian.co.uk (UK site offering tips and links for disabled travellers)

TOURIST INFORMATION

There is just one tourist office in St Petersburg and it is extremely unhelpful. Go only if you want to pick up maps and leaflets.

City Tourist Information Office ⓐ Nevsky pr 41 ⓣ 311 2843
🕐 10.00–19.00 Mon–Fri, 10.00–18.00 Sat.
Also open during the summer on Sundays from 10.00–18.00
Ⓜ Metro: Nevsky Prospekt

BACKGROUND READING

Peter the Great by Robert Massie (Abacus/Ballantine). One of the best biographies of Russia's most powerful tsar, including detailed information on the creation of the city.
Ten Days that Shook the World by John Reed (Penguin). Fascinating eyewitness account of the 1917 Bolshevik power grab. Basis of the film *Reds*.
Crime and Punishment by Fyodor Dostoyevsky (Penguin). Classic St Petersburg fiction. A must-read for any visitor.

Emergencies

POLICE

There are many different branches of the police force, and you are likely to encounter at least one member during your stay. Carry your passport around with you at all times. If you need help, contact your consulate.

Emergency numbers

Ambulance 03
Fire brigade 01
Police 02

HEALTH

The British Embassy has a list of English-speaking doctors. Make sure that you have adequate private travel insurance.

EMERGENCY PHRASES

English	Russian	Pronunciation
Fire!	Пожар!	*pa-zhar!*
Help!	Помогите!	*pa-ma-gi-tye!*
Stop!	Прекратите!	*pri-kra-ti-tye!*
Call a doctor!	Вызовите врача!	*vih-za-vit-ye vra-cha!*
Call the police!	Вызовите милицию!	*vih-za-vit-ye mi-lit-sih-yu!*
Call an ambulance!	Вызовите скорую помощь!	*vih-za-vit-ye sko-ru-yu po-mash!*

Emergency pharmacy

Pharmacies (or *apteka*) are marked by a green cross outside the front door. Most pharmacies open daily from 08.00–21.00.

Hospitals

Hospitals in St Petersburg are extremely poor, but will provide free treatment in the event of an illness. It is more advisable to visit one of the private medical centres that cater to the international community.

American Medical Clinic ⓐ Nab. Reki Moyki 78 ✆ 140 2090
ⓦ www.amclinic.ru Ⓜ Metro: Sadovaya
Euromed Clinic ⓐ Suvorovskiy Prospekt 60 ✆ 327 0301
ⓦ www.euromed.ru Ⓜ Metro: Chernyshevskaya
Hospital #20 ⓐ Gastello St. 21 ✆ 708 4810 Ⓜ Metro: Moskovskaya

LOST PROPERTY

If you lose anything or suspect that it has been stolen, then go straight to the police station near where the incident occurred. You will need a translator if you don't speak Russian.

CONSULATES & EMBASSIES

British Consulate ⓐ pl. Proletarskoy diktatury 5 ✆ 320 3245
ⓦ www.britain.spb.ru 🕓 09.30–13.00, 14.00–17.30 Mon–Fri
New Zealand Embassy ⓐ Povarskaya ul. 44, Moscow ✆ 495 956
3579 ⓦ www.nzembassy.msk.ru 🕓 09.00–17.30 Mon–Fri
US Consulate ⓐ Furshtatskaya ul. 15 ✆ 331 2600
ⓦ www.usconsulate.spb.ru 🕓 09.30–13.30 Mon–Fri

SPOT A CITY IN SECONDS

This great range of pocket city guides will have you in the know in no time. Lightweight and packed with detail on the most important things from shopping and sights to non-stop nightlife, they knock spots off chunkier, clunkier versions. Titles include:

Amsterdam	Bratislava	Glasgow	Madrid	Salzburg
Antwerp	Bruges	Gothenburg	Marrakech	Sarajevo
Athens	Brussels	Granada	Milan	Seville
Barcelona	Bucharest	Hamburg	Monte Carlo	Sofia
Belfast	Budapest	Hanover	Munich	Stockholm
Belgrade	Cardiff	Helsinki	Naples	Strasbourg
Berlin	Cologne	Hong Kong	New York	St Petersburg
Bilbao	Copenhagen	Istanbul	Nice	Tallinn
Bologna	Cork	Kiev	Oslo	Turin
	Dubai	Krakow	Palermo	Valencia
	Dublin	Leipzig	Palma	Venice
	Dubrovnik	Lille	Paris	Verona
	Dusseldorf	Lisbon	Prague	Vienna
	Edinburgh	Ljubljana	Porto	Vilnius
	Florence	London	Reykjavik	Warsaw
	Frankfurt	Lyon	Riga	Zagreb
	Gdansk		Rome	Zurich
	Geneva			
	Genoa			

Available from all good bookshops, your local Thomas Cook travel store or browse and buy on-line at www.thomascookpublishing.com

Thomas Cook Publishing

The publishers would like to thank the following individuals and organisations for providing their copyright photographs for this book:

Pictures Colour Library pages 9, 43; World Pictures page 15; Jon Smith page 122; all the rest, Neil Setchfield.

Copy editor: Penny Isaac
Proofreader: Ian Faulkner

Send your thoughts to
books@thomascook.com

- Found a great bar, club, shop or must-see sight that we don't feature?

- Like to tip us off about any information that needs updating?

- Want to tell us what you love about this handy little guidebook and more importantly how we can make it even handier?

Then here's your chance to tell all! Send us ideas, discoveries and recommendations today and then look out for your valuable input in the next edition of this title. As an extra 'thank you' from Thomas Cook Publishing, you'll be automatically entered into our exciting prize draw.

Send an email to the above address (stating the book's title) or write to: CitySpots Project Editor, Thomas Cook Publishing, PO Box 227, The Thomas Cook Business Park, Unit 18, Coningsby Road, Peterborough PE3 8SB, UK.